Eastern Idaho
SWEET SPOTS

Second edition

Hiking, biking, skiing & climbing

Skiers enjoy the deep snows of Alaska Basin in South Teton Canyon.

Eastern Idaho
SWEET SPOTS

Second edition

Hiking, biking, skiing & climbing

Jerry Painter & Matt TeNgaio

TRAIL GUIDE BOOKS

Published by
Trail Guide Books
P.O. Box 148
Weiser, Idaho 83672

Manufactured in the United States

Maps and topos by Jerry Painter and Matt TeNgaio
Cover and book design by Jerry Painter and Matt TeNgaio
All photographs by the authors, unless otherwise noted
Cover photograph: One of the Granite Basin Lakes at the top of the South Leigh Canyon Trail.

ISBN 978-0-9664233-6-5

A word about safety

It is important to take the proper precautions in all outdoor activities. It is impossible to alert you to every hazard or anticipate all the limitations of every reader or group in a guidebook. Because of this, the descriptions of trails, routes and natural features in this book do not necessarily mean that a particular place or trip or climb will be safe for your group.

It also helps to remember that to fully enjoy many of the trails described in this book a certain level of physical conditioning is required – especially trails, rides or climbs rated as strenuous.

When you follow any of the trips or climbs described in this book, you assume responsibility for the safety of yourself or your party. Under all conditions, excursions require that you pay the proper attention to driving conditions, traffic, roads, trails, weather, terrain, the capabilities of your group members and other factors.

It is also important to remember that the lands described in this book are subject to development and ownership changes. Access and other conditions may have changed since this book was published that may make it unwise to use the exact routes described. Always check for current conditions ahead of time, respect posted private property signs, and avoid confrontations with property owners or managers. We have provided information sources in this book. You are also welcome to contact the authors directly. Staying informed on current conditions and using common sense are the best ways to enjoy fun and safe outings.

Another warning: Climbing involves an element of risk, as do all outdoor activities discussed in this book. Climbing (and other outdoor activities) can be deadly. Learn how to climb from competent instructors and always use safe climbing habits and equipment. People have been seriously hurt and killed in climbing areas described in this book. Remember that problems usually arise from poor judgment, poor communication, improper equipment and bad belaying practices. Be safe.

Acknowledgements

A lot of people helped make this information possible. We would like to thank the many people who went on hiking, skiing, biking and climbing trips with us. We would like to thank our wives, Julie and Brittany for putting up with our obsessions of being outdoors and for often tagging along. A thanks goes out to Dean Lords, Greg Collins, Jim Olson, Marc Hanselman and Steve Reiser for information on the local climbing crags. Thanks to the Forest Service and Bureau of Land Management for information and advice. Thanks to all those who got in front of our cameras to provide us with useful photos. If there are any goof ups, blame us and tell us about them. We'll try to get them fixed in the next go around.

Locations
covered in book

🚶 Hiking		⛷ Skiing	
🚲 Biking		🧗 Climbing	

15

Island
Park

20

Ashton

28

Rexburg

33

N Howe

Idaho
Falls

20

26

Swan Valley

26

15

Blackfoot

86

Pocatello

IDAHO

WYOMING

Detail
area

CONTENTS

Skiing trails

Climbing areas

Introduction

It's a common question, "Where's a good place to ...?" Fill in the blank with hike, bike, ski, snowshoe, rock climb, peak bag, etc. Fortunately for those who live in eastern Idaho, there are lots of good answers to that question. Within a few hours of town, you can be in world-class backcountry. This is country that people come from across the continent to vacation in. It's cool living so close.

This book focuses on the outdoor activities and tells you where the sweet spots are. It is not comprehensive. Generally speaking, it fills in some of the gaps that exist in the book "Trails of Eastern Idaho" by Margaret Fuller and Jerry Painter. Think of it as a companion to "Trails of Eastern Idaho." Because that book is confined to Idaho, many great trails and areas are left out that are just across the border in Wyoming.

However, in this second edition of Sweet Spots, four new climbing areas and a handful of high quality mountain bikes trails have been added to the bounty of trails and crags already documented in the first edition.

We hope that when you buy your mountain bike, a pair of climbing shoes or cross-country skis that you'll also pick up a copy of this book. You may as well know where all the best places are to play with your new toys. This book is the most up-to-date and accurate guide to rock climbing areas from Pocatello to Driggs to Howe. It includes some of the best mountain bike rides in the area. You'll find a full winter's worth of ski trails to explore. If it's hiking you crave, we'll turn you on to trails you'll remember for the rest of your life. One helpful hint: While our maps are useful and often all you'll need, we encourage you to take along a set of Forest service and/or BLM maps for greater detail of the areas you'll be in. At the very least, they can be helpful driving to the right starting point.

These are some of the sweetest spots for recreating in eastern Idaho and, in some cases, the western states.

A dayhiker sits above School Room Glacier at Hurricane Pass in the Tetons.

HIKING

HIDDEN LAKE LOOP

GETTING THERE: From Rexburg, Idaho, drive north on Highway 20 about 5 miles and turn east on Highway 33. Drive east on Highway 33 for about 16 miles and turn north on Highway 32. If you come to the town of Tetonia, you've gone too far. Follow this highway to mile marker 11 and turn north (right) on 4700 E. Go one mile and turn east (right) on 4600 E (also called Coyote Meadows Road). There should be a sign for Coyote Meadows. Follow this road for about three miles where it enters the national forest and becomes FR 265. Folow this road until it ends at the Coyote Meadows trailhead.

DISTANCE: 4.5 miles to Hidden Lake; 6.5 miles to Conant Basin; about 18 miles for the loop around to North Bitch Creek and back to Coyote Meadows.

DIFFICULTY: Moderate to Hidden Lake and Conant Basin; a bit harder around to North Bitch Creek.

WHEN TO GO: All summer and early fall. This area is used by hunters in late fall. Access roads can be poor to impassable after heavy rains or snows.

The trail up to Hidden Lake from Coyote Meadows gains only about 900 feet in 4.5 miles. That makes it a perfect beginner backpacker trail, day hike or a good trail to get your horse into shape on.

Whenever the trail does climb, the route uses well-made switchbacks and gradual slopes. If you're in shape, you can pretty much go on cruise control most of the way up.

The trail climbs through a mix of forest, mostly lodgepole pine with some fir and aspen mixed in. The first mile follows Coyote Creek then heads up a ridge across the wilderness boundary. There are a few intermittent streams along the way, but many of them dry up later in the year.

Hidden Lake is just a few acres large. It's completely surrounded by timber. In years past there have been some nice-sized trout of the 1 to 2 pound variety in the lake. Remember that you'll need a Wyoming fishing license to legally fish. Hidden Lake is under special camping restrictions — no camping with stock animals or stock grazing.

About one-fourth mile past the lake, the trail comes to Crystal Spring. There is a nice campsite here with a bear proof food box. The large spring provides good water for nearby campers. There are no restrictions for this area.

Most of the trail is inside the Jedediah Smith Wilderness Area. Bikes and motorized vehicles are prohibited inside the wilderness.

The trail continues on to Conant Basin to the northwest. From here the trail forks; one trail goes east over Jackass Pass into Teton National Park and the southern route heads south and loops back to the Coyote Meadows Trailhead.

Jackass Pass is reputed to be the same route taken by John Colter — one of the first white men to enter Jackson Hole — as he headed south in the early 1800s.

11

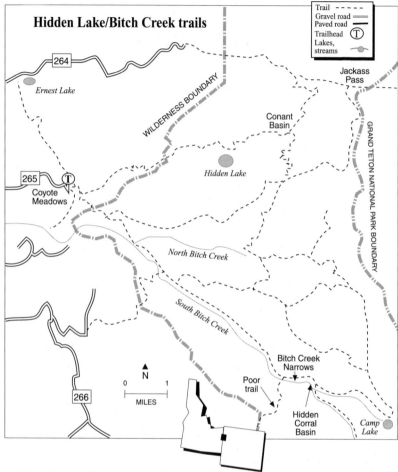

Hidden Lake/Bitch Creek trails

Trail - - - -
Gravel road ═══
Paved road ▬▬▬
Trailhead (T)
Lakes, streams

264

Ernest Lake

WILDERNESS BOUNDARY

Jackass Pass

Conant Basin

Hidden Lake

265

Coyote Meadows

GRAND TETON NATIONAL PARK BOUNDARY

North Bitch Creek

South Bitch Creek

Bitch Creek Narrows

N
0   1
MILES

266

Poor trail

Hidden Corral Basin

Camp Lake

Keep in mind if you are camping, that this area is only 10 miles from the Yellowstone National Park border and considered grizzly bear country. Many of the campsites in this area have bear proof boxes or bear poles for hanging your gear. If you camp where there are no boxes or poles already set up, then you should hang your foodstuffs in a bag from a tree limb at least 10 feet off the ground, eat away from your sleeping area and never take food into your tent.

Dayhikers or horseback riders will rarely see any bears. They usually see or hear you first.

HIDDEN CORRAL BASIN / SOUTH BITCH CREEK

GETTING THERE: From Rexburg, Idaho, drive north on Highway 20 about

5 miles and turn east on Highway 33. Drive east on Highway 33 for about 16 miles and turn north on Highway 32. If you come to the town of Tetonia, you've gone too far. Follow this highway to mile marker 11 and turn north (right) on 4700 E. Go one mile and turn east (right) on 4600 E (also called Coyote Meadows Road). There should be a sign for Coyote Meadows. Follow this road for about three miles where it enters the national forest and becomes FR 265. Folow this road until it ends at the Coyote Meadows trailhead.

DISTANCE: It's about 7.25 miles to the Bitch Creek Narrows and another mile beyond to Hidden Corral Basin. It's close to 2 miles from Hidden Corral Basin to Camp Lake.

DIFFICULTY: Moderate – mostly because of distance – up to the narrows and the basin; beyond the basin the trail climbs steeply up to Camp Lake, less steeper up to the creek's headwaters.

WHEN TO GO: June to October for hiking and horseback riding; skiers would need a ride in from snowmobilers to access the trails in winter. Roads can be poor after a heavy rain or snow. This area is used heavily by hunters in the fall.

One of the most beautiful spots in the Tetons is a gorgeous basin about 8 miles up the South Bitch Creek canyon.

Hidden Corral Basin is so named because it was used by horse thieves around the turn of the century to hide their stolen stock. About 7 miles up from Coyote Meadows, the canyon narrows abruptly. With a few poles stretched across the narrows, livestock were kept safely for weeks in a natural corral until buyers could be found.

Nowadays the canyon and basin are perfect getaways for backpackers and horseback riders looking for some solitude. All but the first mile of the trail is inside the Jedediah Smith Wilderness Area. Bikes and motorized vehicles are prohibited inside the wilderness.

The narrows section forces the creek through several stretches of beautiful cascades and drops. It is especially pretty during high water runoff years in the Tetons.

There are some nice campsites in the basin; a bear proof box is also available.

The hike up from Coyote Meadows requires a stream crossing and has a few ups and downs in the beginning, but for the most part is fairly level, easy trekking. Except for the distances, it's not too tough.

Beyond Hidden Corral Basin, the trail forks. The trail heading south follows the creek and eventually connects into South Badger Creek. The fork heading east climbs up to Camp Lake, then turns north to connect into a series of ridgeline trails. The area around Camp Lake is restricted camping – no livestock grazing allowed. The headwaters of South Bitch Creek is also a restricted camping zone.

GREEN LAKES

GETTING THERE: Drive 5.5 miles north of Driggs, Idaho on Highway 33. When the highway makes a 90-degree turn west, continue going straight. Take the next road right (east) — there are signs to North and South Leigh Creek trails. The road soon becomes gravel. Drive 2.5 miles and turn left (north) at the sign for North Leigh Creek. Drive about 5 miles to the end of the road and a parking area at the trailhead.

Dayhikers work on lunch at the first Green Lake in the Tetons.

14

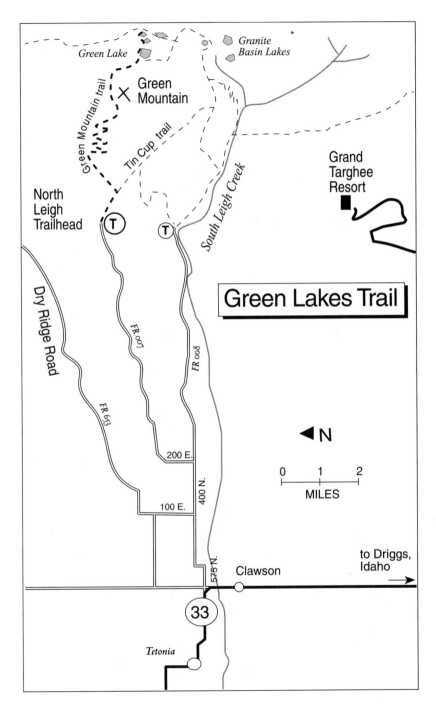

Green Lake

Granite Basin Lakes

Green Mountain

Green Mountain trail

Tin Cup trail

South Leigh Creek

Grand Targhee Resort

North Leigh Trailhead

Green Lakes Trail

Dry Ridge Road

FR 007

FR 008

FR 653

◀ N

200 E.

100 E.

400 N.

575 N.

0   1   2
MILES

to Driggs, Idaho

Clawson

33

Tetonia

15

DISTANCE: 12.5 miles round-trip to the first lake. Add another 2 miles if you go farther up the canyon to other lakes.
DIFFICULTY: Strenuous. Gains about 2,000 feet in the first 4 miles.
SEASON: July to October. Snow can linger into midsummer on the ridge next to Green Mountain.

This is beautiful wilderness hiking in the upper west side of the Teton range. The trail seems to have it all. The Green Lakes hike is a good all-day hike or overnight backpacking trip.

The trail crosses a footbridge over Tin Cup Creek and almost immediately enters the Jedediah Smith Wilderness Area. The trail quickly begins its uphill climb to the Green Mountain Ridge. Most of the trail is well made. The grades are not too steep, and switchbacks help manage the climb up the side of the mountain.

For the first mile the trail takes you through thick lodgepole and fir forest. There are also some huckleberries to watch for in late summer.

As the trail climbs higher, it takes you through some patches of aspens. Soon the trail begins some wide switchbacks through open treeless areas. The wildflowers here are superb, especially in mid- to late-July.

After about four miles of steady climbing and switchbacking, the trail reaches a ridge and levels off for about .25-miles. This is as high as you'll get on the way to the lakes. Snow often lingers on this ridge until midsummer.

The trail drops down the northeast side of the ridge in a series of switchbacks that go on for about .5 miles. Within another half-mile you arrive at the first Green Lake.

Look for trout and osprey in and above the lake. There is a good campsite on the northeast side of the lake.

There are three more lakes above the first. All three are within about 1.5 miles from the first. These other lakes are about half the size of the first lake.

The return trip is fairly easy once you get past the steep switchbacks on the northeast side of the ridge.

SOUTH LEIGH CREEK/GRANITE BASIN LAKES

GETTING THERE: From Driggs, Idaho, drive 5.5 miles north on Highway 33. As the highway takes a 90-degree turn to the left (west), turn off the highway, continuing north. Turn right (east) at the next road. There should be signs for North and South Leigh trails. The road soon becomes gravel. Continue on this road for 7 miles to the trailhead.
DISTANCE: 1.4 miles to the Andy Stone Trail junction; 2.7 miles to the next trail junction; 4 miles to the switchbacks; and 7.7 miles to Granite Basin.
HOW STRENUOUS: Mostly easy for the first 4 miles from the trailhead to the switchbacks. Strenuous up the switchbacks to Granite Basin (about 2,500 feet gain from the creek bottom to Granite Basin in 3 miles).
SEASON: June to October if you only want to hike the creek bottom; late June or early July to October for Granite Basin.
SPECIAL CONSIDERATIONS: Watch out for stinging nettle along the creek. Snow lingers in Granite Basin until after July 4 most years.

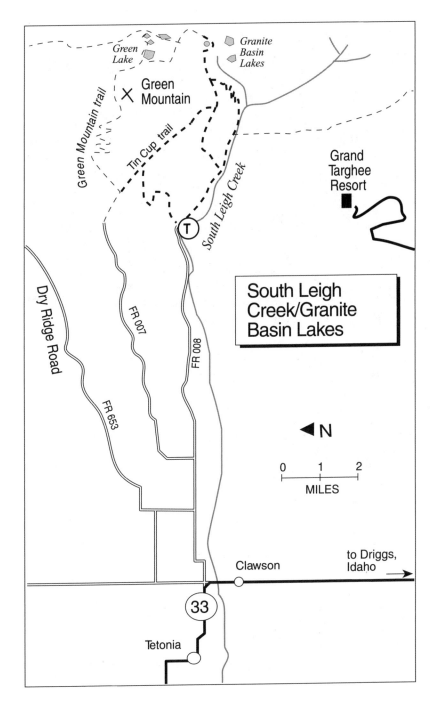

Green Lake

Granite Basin Lakes

Green Mountain

Green Mountain trail

Tin Cup trail

South Leigh Creek

(T)

Grand Targhee Resort

South Leigh Creek/Granite Basin Lakes

Dry Ridge Road

FR 007

FR 008

FR 653

◀ N

0   1   2
MILES

to Driggs, Idaho →

Clawson

33

Tetonia

One of the pretty alpine lakes in Granite Basin on the west side of the Tetons.

This is a trail with a split personality. The first four miles that parallel South Leigh Creek are gentle and easy walking. But if you are interested in taking off out of the canyon, get ready to huff and puff. These trails climb nearly to the top of the range.

This canyon has more streams than are shown on the map. The trail crosses three good-sized streams the first 1.3 miles before you reach the Andy Stone Trail Junction. Most of these streams flow through midsummer, but by late August, some are only muddy spots. Because this is a wet area, be prepared to battle mosquitoes and biting flies.

The canyon is heavily forested with fir and spruce. The trail passes through occasional meadows that are a mass of wild flowers in mid summer.

The trail only draws near the main creek a few times. If you wish to wade or fish the stream, there are a couple of nice places about three miles down the trail and near the junction with the trail to Teton Creek. At this junction there is a large stock/foot bridge over the creek.

If you wish to spend the night, there is a large campsite at the bottom of the switchbacks. There also are some other nice spots at the meadows before the foot-bridge.

At the top of the canyon await beautiful alpine basin lakes and views to rival any in the Tetons. On the hike up you will see the Grand Teton towering over the ridge. These lakes once boasted trout, but now appear to be empty. The three largest lakes are from three to five acres in size. Beautiful snowmelt creeks cascade down the surrounding cliffs to fill the lakes each spring.

There are two routes to see the Granite Basin Lakes. Both are strenuous and it depends on how you like your poison: all at once or spread out. The Andy Stone Trail climbs right up the side of the canyon with only a few level stretches to let you catch your breath. The other route, a switchback trail at the end of the canyon,

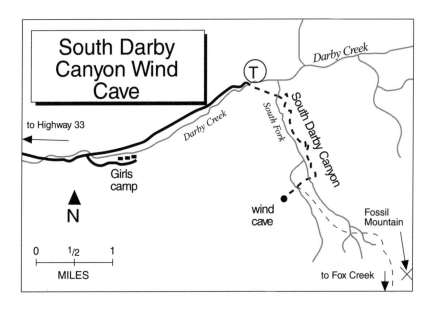

seems to take forever to get you to the top. But the switchbacks are well engineered so as not to bite off huge elevation gains at each turn.

SOUTH DARBY CANYON / WIND CAVE

GETTING THERE: From Victor, Idaho, drive 5.5 miles north on Highway 33. Turn right (east) onto a paved road. Look for signs at the beginning of the road for Darby Girls Camp. After a mile the road becomes gravel. After another half mile the road forks. Go right and follow this road about 6 miles to its end, where you may park.

DISTANCE: 3.4 miles to Wind Cave.

HOW STRENUOUS: Gains 1,800 feet, moderately strenuous, but a well-made trail.

WHEN TO GO: Mid-June to October for hiking.

SPECIAL CONSIDERATIONS: Bring headlamp or flashlights for cave.

This is a fun trail with a super destination. The wind cave at the end of the trail adds an extra bit of fascination to a hike with nice waterfalls and scenery.

This trail is often called the "Monument Hike" by locals because of a cement and rock monument placed in the upper basin, near the wind cave. The monument is in remembrance of five people who died here after being struck by lightning during a thunderstorm. The group consisted of hikers from the nearby summer girls camp.

The trail starts off with a footbridge across Darby Creek, then begins to climb away from the creek. After about a half of a mile, the trail enters the Jedediah Smith Wilderness and crosses the South Fork of Darby Creek.

19

Hiking down from a visit to the South Darby Canyon wind cave.

After crossing the creek, the trail climbs sharply up the canyon. Most of the tough part of the trail comes in the next 1.5 miles. The last mile climbs at a less-drastic incline.

An interesting phenomenon is that the creek disappears underground for a short way about a mile up the canyon. Late in the season, the creek is often dry until you reach the cave where a small stream flows from the cave's mouth.

The trail continues to climb with a few switchbacks until it is near the canyon rim and into some less-forested terrain. Along this point watch the opposite rim for waterfalls. Late in the season, these can be somewhat diminished or nonexistent.

As the trail approaches the upper basin, it enters a thickly forested area and turns west. Before entering the trees you should be able to see the wind cave along the western wall of the canyon.

Below the cave are some campsites for backpackers.

The trail forks just before you arrive at the monument. The fork heading up the basin along the creek is not shown on some maps. This unmaintained use trail goes up to the base of Fossil Mountain and drops into Fox Creek Canyon.

From the monument, it's a steep hike up switchbacks to the mouth of the wind cave. During wet, cooler years, snow often lingers around the cave into midsummer. Make sure you bring along flashlights or headlamps to safely enjoy the interior of the cave. On hot days the gusts of wind coming from the cave feel like a giant air conditioner. The cave is really a natural tunnel with wind pouring through from inlets farther up the canyon. The cave goes deep into the mountain and comes out at about the same level along the ridge about .75 miles up the canyon. Between the entrance and exit are some 40-foot drops and climbs that require ropes and caving skills to negotiate.

ALASKA BASIN

GETTING THERE: From Victor, Idaho, drive 8 miles north on Highway 33 to Driggs. Turn right (east) at the main intersection, and follow the signs to Grand

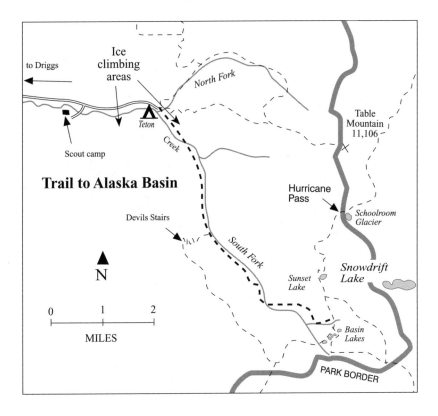

Trail to Alaska Basin

Targhee Ski Resort. Drive 6 miles and turn right onto a paved road with a sign for Teton Campground. After a few hundred feet the road turns to dirt. Drive 5 miles to the trailhead/parking lot for South Teton Creek Trail.

DISTANCE: 8 miles one way to the basin lakes; another 2.5 miles up to the top of Hurricane Pass.

DIFFICULTY: Moderately strenuous for the last 3 miles with an elevation gain of 2,400 feet to the basin lakes.

WHEN TO GO: Late June to October. The trail is usually snow covered through May.

SPECIAL CONSIDERATIONS: If you're backpacking, bring a pack stove. Campfires are not allowed in the basin lakes area.

This is one of the most heavily used trails on the west side of the Tetons, next to the Table (Rock) Mountain trail. What makes the trail so popular is its magical beauty from the lower parts of the canyon all the way to the captivating basin lakes.

Because of its popularity, it is well-maintained and has foot bridges over the major stream crossings.

From the trailhead, the path immediately enters the Jedediah Smith Wilderness. The most striking features in the first few miles are the wonderful wildflowers and the lively creek, that has some stretches where it cascades and drops.

At about 3.5 miles, the trail forks. The trail to the right heads up Devils Stairs.

Alpine setting of Alaska Basin is dominated by Buck Mountain to the east.

This strenuous trail (not recommended for horses) switchbacks up to a large hanging shelf on the canyon's southwest side. It offers nice views of the canyon below and the surrounding peaks.

The main South Fork trail continues up the canyon alongside the creek through heavily forested terrain.

At about mile 7, you'll pass through some campsite areas. These larger campsites are popular with horsepackers, who are not allowed to camp in the fragile basin lakes area.

At about 7.5 miles, the trail switchbacks over a ridge and into Alaska Basin. Historians believe this beautiful rocky basin was named by settlers who returned from the Alaskan gold rush.

Look for the bold marmots that inhabit the basin. Remember to hang your food away from marmots and other camp robbers, such as bears.

From Alaska Basin, there are routes in several directions in the range. To get to Hurricane Pass, follow the well-marked trails north to Sunset Lake and the pass. A strenuous .6 mile trail takes you to this beautiful alpine lake with limited campsites. From the lake it's another two miles to the top of Hurricane Pass. The pass offers one of the more memorable sights of the Grand Teton, Middle Teton, South Teton and Schoolroom Glacier.

FOX CREEK

GETTING THERE: Three miles north of Victor, turn east on the Fox Creek Road. Drive 4 miles to the end of the road and park.

The Fox Creek Trail starts out near a rock quarry that is on private property. Some of the first section follows the entrance road into the quarry. Signs lead hikers and horseback riders off the road and onto the south side of the creek to a rocky foot path. There is one sign near the beginning of the trail that says "Fox Creek

22

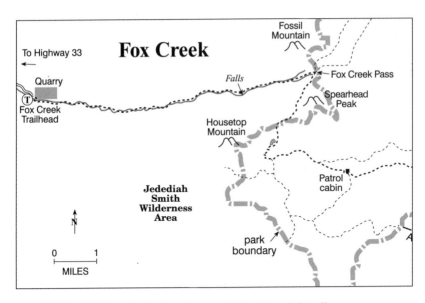

Pass 10." Don't believe it. At best, the pass is less than eight miles up.

The first five miles up the canyon are mostly easy-going and gentle in elevation gain. The trail travels through lush forest. There are several stream crossings; most are easy to negotiate in late summer and fall. Earlier in the year, hikers will probably want to bring along sandals to slip into for the stream crossings.

After about five miles the trail begins to get more serious in elevation gain. From the trailhead to Fox Creek Pass — about 8 miles — the trail gains a moderate 3,000 feet. At mile five, look for pretty Fox Creek Falls streaming over a rock cliff. These falls are marked on the Jedediah Smith and Winegar Hole Wilderness Map available at the Forest Service office. The falls will be below the trail on the right side.

Above the falls, the trail continues to climb. On your left (north) side of the canyon, Fossil Mountain comes into view. Fossil Mountain is 10,950 feet. As you get closer to the base of the peak, you will notice a prominent notch on the west side between the peak and the canyon rim. This "pass" has a rough trail that leads to the top of South Darby Canyon.

The upper two miles of Fox Creek Canyon offer a few nice campsites.

Just before Fox Creek Pass is a junction with the Teton Crest Trail. Here is where the views become wonderful. To the northeast are the Teton's tallest peaks, including the Grand Teton. To the south is Housetop Mountain and Spearhead Peak.

At this junction you have options of heading south to Marion Lake and the top of Granite Canyon about 1.8 miles away or east down Death Canyon or north along the Death Canyon Shelf toward Alaska Basin.

GAME CREEK

GETTING THERE: Finding the Game Creek trailhead can be a bit tricky.

23

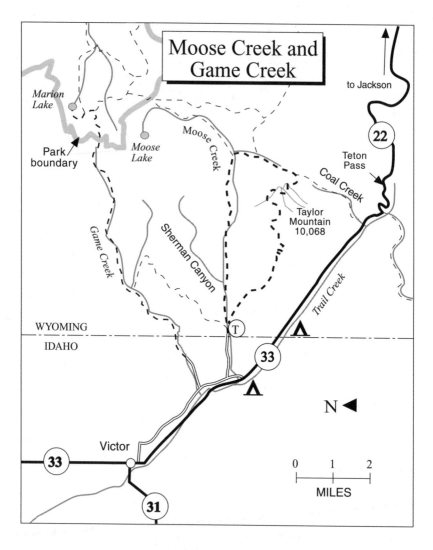

About five miles southeast of Victor on state Highway 33, turn east at the sign that says Moose Creek and take an immediate left. After a few hundred feet, the road passes the Moose Creek Road with a large sign pointing to the trailhead. Continue north about one mile and look for a cluster of houses. Turn right (east) on a road between the homes (find the one that doesn't end up being a driveway). Take this road to the end. Near the end of the road, keep left at the intersection and park in an open area just below an irrigation headgate on the creek.

The trail starts on the north side of the creek. You can walk across the bridge at the headgate. On the other side is a sign indicating that the Grand Teton National Park boundary is 6.9 miles up the trail.

24

Dayhikers soak up the views at the top of Game Creek canyon.

The trail up Game Creek is easy going, except for the stream crossings. A couple of the stream crossings have nice fat logs to skip across on, but higher up the trail, you may be forced to take off our boots and wade across. Consider taking a lightweight pair of sandals for these wet crossings. If you go earlier in the summer when the water is higher and swifter, walking sticks are recommended.

The creek begins to do a disappearing act around the 5.5 mile area. The creek goes underground for 100 yards or so, then re-emerges above ground.

Around the 6-mile mark, the trail occasionally does a disappearing act. In places where the trail passes through meadows, grass sometimes fills in the path. If you lose the trail, don't worry too much. If you walk parallel to the creek (on the south side), the trail eventually reappears.

At the top of the canyon, the trail has generous switchbacks to help you climb up to the crest of the Tetons. The route tops out at 10,200 feet. On the ridge you are presented with some nice views of the southern end of the range.

MOOSE CREEK

GETTING THERE: From Victor, Idaho, drive 3 miles southeast on Highway 33 and turn left on the Moose Creek Road; drive .3 miles and turn right (east) and drive to the end of the road and park.

DISTANCE: 4.4 miles up to Moose Meadows; 5.8 miles to the falls; 8 miles to Moose Lake.

HOW STRENUOUS: Mostly easy, gains 800 feet to meadows.

SEASON: Late May to October.

SPECIAL CONSIDERATIONS: The water is clear and shallow making it easy to spook the trout.

25

Moose Creek falls.

The Moose Creek Trail offers a fun hike up a classic mountain canyon featuring a good-sized trout stream, beaver ponds, a large meadow, waterfall and small lake.

This trail takes you into the Jedediah Smith Wilderness Area. The trail starts out tough for the first 1/8 of a mile until it climbs up to an old dirt road along the south side of the creek. From here the next mile or so is fairly easy hiking. The road eventually narrows down to a trail. The canyon is thickly forested with Douglas fir, spruce and lodgepole pine. Willow brush clogs the creek bottoms.

The trail crosses the creek on a nice footbridge at the second mile. If at first you don't spot the bridge, keep looking. The horseback riders usually walk through the water. After the bridge, the trail climbs sharply for a quarter of a mile. At the three-mile mark is a small meadow fed by a spring and backed up by some busy beavers.

At 4.4 miles up the canyon, the trail comes to Moose Meadows. This huge meadow is several acres wide. The area is laced with beaver channels and slack water.

There are a few campsites at the meadows.

Past the meadows the trail begins a steady uphill. Just past the meadows, the trail crosses the creek. There is no bridge here, so plan on getting wet feet.

Another 1.4 miles up the trail is a nice waterfall. When the trail takes you through a rocky section, watch the creek canyon from the trail for a narrow gap that the water falls through.

Grand Teton National Park is about 1.7 miles from the falls. The trail forks about .5-miles before the park boundary. The trail following the creek hooks west and leads up to beautiful Moose Lake. If you wish to camp at the lake, bring a pack stove. No fires are allowed around the lake.

INDIAN CREEK

GETTING THERE: Drive 19 miles southeast of Swan Valley on Highway 26 and turn left (east) into the middle of a wide canyon with a sign marked "Indian Creek." Follow the good gravel road for about 2 miles and turn right at the fork to go to the South Fork trailhead or left at the fork to go to the North Fork trailhead. There are some nice car camping sites along this road. This road can be slippery and mucky after a heavy rain. Two miles from the fork, you come to a trailhead parking area, kiosk, pit toilet and area for off-loading horses.

DISTANCE: About 8 miles from the South Fork trailhead to above the lake basin area. About 6.5 miles from the North Fork trailhead to the top of the canyon.

DIFFICULTY: Easy for the first 2 miles; strenuous in the upper canyon.

BEST TIME TO GO: Late June to October.

The Indian Creek trail starts out right on the Idaho border and climbs east into some super backcountry.

Indian Creek has two main canyons – north and south – that are heavily forested and deep. Fir, spruce, pine, cottonwood and aspen are thick throughout the lower reaches of the canyon. The trail takes you high into the lower reaches of the Snake River Range. Many of the peaks along the canyon and near the lake basin are close to 10,000 feet high.

If you are on horseback or are a fast hiker, you can connect the two canyons via

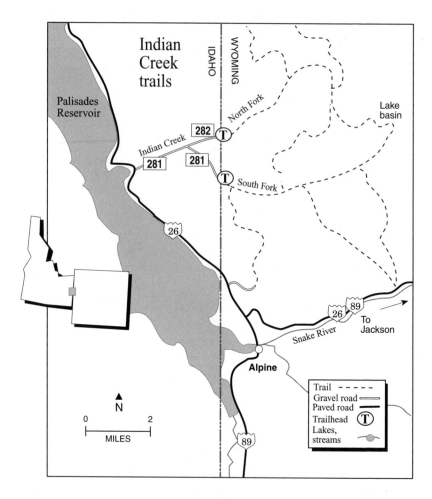

Indian Creek trails

Palisades Reservoir

IDAHO | WYOMING

North Fork

282 (T)

Indian Creek

281 | 281

(T) South Fork

Lake basin

26

26 89

To Jackson

Snake River

Alpine

Trail - - - - -
Gravel road =
Paved road ▬▬▬
Trailhead (T)
Lakes, streams ●

N

0   2

MILES

89

some passes at the top of the canyons. This area also makes an enjoyable overnight trip. There are some nice campsites in the lake basin or near Deadhorse Canyon. Be aware that the area is visited regularly by hunters in the fall. The trail is open to motorbikes and snowmobiles. Mountain bikers will find the first two to three miles enjoyable, but it gets very tough after that.

The first four miles up the South Fork are very picturesque and mostly easy. The trail is in pretty good shape. About a mile up, there are a couple of stream crossings without a bridge. A walking stick and a couple of handy logs will get you over dry.

Around the sixth mile, the trail comes to the first of three more stream crossings. The last crossing is not a problem. But the other two can be challenges if the water is high. It may be wisest to just take off your boots and wade through. The water is surprisingly deep high in the canyon — especially during wetter years.

On the way up the canyon are a couple of side canyons with two trails leading south and one heading north. The southern trails climb steeply out of the canyon, over the top and down into canyons that intersect near the east-west flowing Snake River and Highway 26-89. The northern trail climbs up to the north rim of the canyon and follows it over to near the lake basin.

After the sixth mile, the trees begin to thin and most of the hillsides are covered in grass and scrub brush with an occasional wind blasted fir tree. About the seventh mile the trail climbs into a lake basin. This last mile up is steep – gaining about 1,000 feet. The lakes are really large, spring-fed ponds tucked in close to the mountain ridges.

Just before the lake basin is a trail junction. The trail heading east goes down Dog Creek Canyon and eventually down to Highway 26-89 near Hoback, Wyo.

From the lake basin, the trail climbs up and over a 9,000-foot-plus ridge and drops into the North Fork canyon of Indian Creek after winding through two more smaller passes. The head of the canyon is a beautiful alpine mountain cirque.

From the top of the North Fork canyon it's about another 6 miles back to the trailhead, but the walk back along the road to complete the loop is almost another 3 miles. The North Fork canyon is narrower than the South Fork Canyon. If you don't like hiking on dirt roads, you might want to stash a mountain bike at the other trailhead and ride the last three miles back to your vehicle.

SOUTH HORSESHOE CREEK

GETTING THERE: From Idaho Falls, take Highway 20 north past Rexburg and take the exit onto Highway 33 heading east. Drive about 27 miles and turn south on the Powerline Road. Drive 4 miles and turn east on Packsaddle Road. Drive 3 miles east and turn south (don't cross the Teton River). Drive 1 mile south and keep on the main road as it turns southwest. After 2.5 miles you will come to a sign indicating Horseshoe Creek. The trailhead is another 2.5 miles up the road.

DISTANCE: About 3 miles to the top of the first main ridge; 4.5 miles to Elk Flat; about 17.5 miles for a loop down North Fork of Mahogany Creek and back to the trailhead.

ELEVATION: The trailhead is at about 6,000 feet; the first ridge hits 8,000 feet.

HOW STRENUOUS: Easy to the beaver dams, moderate to strenuous up to the first ridge.

WHEN TO GO: June through October most years. Snow often lingers on the north-facing slopes above 8,000 feet. The access roads can be a mess following a heavy rain or snow. This area is heavily hunted during the fall.

The Horseshoe Creek trail is one of those "get away from the crowds" type paths. You may see a few vehicles at the trailhead, but chances are you may never see anyone on the trail.

The trail is open to bikers and foot traffic (bikers should see the Horseshoe Canyon trails in the biking section). There is plenty of parking available about 100 yards from the trailhead for horse trailers.

The trail offers different possibilities depending on how far up the trail you travel. After about 1 mile you come to a series of beaver ponds.

In the next 2 miles, the trail climbs up next to a nameless peak at 8,065 feet.

29

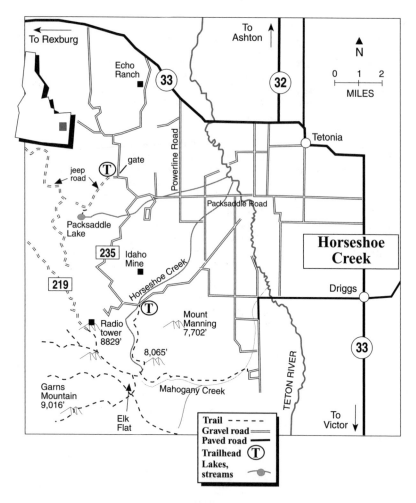

The trail climbs over a ridge and comes to Elk Flat after about 4.5 miles. Before Elk Flat the trail intersects with two other trails. One trail heads northwest to a radio station relay tower and the other goes east down the North Fork of Mahogany Creek. Beyond Elk Flat, the trail climbs up Garns Mountain which stands at 9,016 feet. On a clear day expect some inspiring views of the Teton Mountains. Garns Mountain is a bald, round-topped mountain.

If you're looking for an overnight camping spot, head up to Elk Flat. There is also a trail heading south out of Elk Flat that follows much of the Big Hole Mountains' crest for about 12 miles. The trail ends at Pine Creek Pass on U.S. Highway 31 – the road between Swan Valley and Victor.

These trails take you through some beautiful rugged mountain country. Expect to find some parts of the trail to be a bit beat up by erosion and clogged with downfall.

A hiker skips along the paved Cress Creek Nature Trail.

CRESS CREEK NATURE TRAIL

GETTING THERE: Take U.S. Highway 26 east out of Idaho Falls, go about 14 miles and turn left, follow the signs to Heise and Kelly Canyon Ski area. Immediately after you cross the bridge over the Snake River, turn left. Go about 1.5 miles to the parking area.

DISTANCE: About 2 miles round-trip.

DIFFICULTY: Mostly easy.

SEASON: April to November.

SPECIAL CONSIDERATIONS: If you time your visit in the evening, you'll be treated to an awesome sunset on clear summer days.

The Cress Creek Nature Trail is like an old friend to many hikers in eastern Idaho.

But like some old friends who have gone off to the city and returned with an uptown personality, the Cress Creek Nature Trail has changed radically in recent years.

In 2003, this trail near Heise has had major improvement work done on it. The parking lot at the trailhead was expanded and now boasts a restroom. The once crumbling banks have been pushed back and shielded with chain-link fence. Perhaps the most major change is the cement sidewalk that gradually climbs the hill making the first half mile of trail wheelchair accessible. Work on Cress Creek Nature Trail continues.

The trail still follows the same general route of the former trail, only it takes its time with gentle switchbacks up the Snake River canyon side. Walkers can short-cut some of the switchbacks via stairs.

31

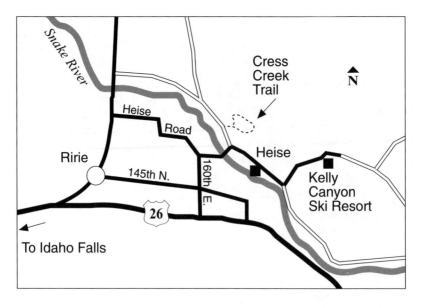

Along the first half mile are large metal signs that combine history, geology and natural facts about the surroundings. Pay attention to one sign in particular, there is a serious test later on up the trail.

The higher you climb, the better the views get. At the end of the paved section of trail, the route continues along a gravel road. As the road begins to go downhill, look for a dirt trail on your left. Take this uphill trail. This is part of the old Cress Creek Trail that makes a large loop higher up the hillside and follows along the creek. This loop trail adds another mile onto the entire route. If you continue down the gravel road you'll end up back at the river road that you drove in on.

Most of the area is high-country desert — sage brush, scrubby trees, lava rock and a few cactus — until the trail reaches the creek. Here, you enter lush growth with thick green, leafy foliage. The small stream is clogged with water cress. If you read the signs at the start of the trail, you'll also be able to identify one of the most dangerous denizens of the backcountry: Poison ivy. This nasty plant stands guard near the trail and along the stream area. Make sure the kids know how to identify it.

The trail features nice overlook views of the Snake River valley to the west and some of the Snake River canyon to the south and east. On clear days you can see Big Southern Butte and the mountain ranges to the west.

Perhaps the best time to hike this trail is close to dusk. With the setting sun back lighting the distant mountains and valley you can make out the Lost River and Lemhi mountain ranges.

There is a faint trail off the upper part of the loop trail that leads to the top of the canyon ridge. A radio tower is visible at the ridge top. This route is more of a workout and adds another mile or so onto the total distance.

There is a variety of wildlife that inhabits the area. Some include rabbits, ground squirrels, snakes, lizards, deer, eagles, osprey, foxes and several kinds of song birds.

A marmot peaks out from under a boulder in the Tetons.

Peak bagging

TABLE (ROCK) MOUNTAIN

GETTING THERE: From Victor, Idaho, drive 8 miles north on Highway 33 to Driggs. Turn right (east) at the main intersection, following the signs to Grand Targhee Ski Resort, drive 6 miles, and turn right onto a paved road with a sign for Teton Campground. This road soon becomes gravel. Drive 5 miles to the trailhead/parking lot for North Teton Creek Trail, or continue down the road to the South Teton Creek Trailhead.

DISTANCE: 12.5 miles roundtrip if you take the North Fork trail; 9 miles roundtrip if you take the ridge route from the South Fork parking lot.

HOW STRENUOUS: The trail gains 4,100 feet from trailhead to summit. It's a lot more enjoyable if you're in good shape.

SEASON: Early July most years, to October. March to April as a ski climb.

SPECIAL CONSIDERATIONS: If you don't mind the cold, April can be a good time to climb the peak. Go on mornings when the temperatures are cold

From the left, Mount Owens, the Grand Teton and Table Mountain.

enough to keep the snow solid to avoid post holing. The temperatures can be as much as 20 degrees colder on the summit than the valley floor. Bring along a jacket.

Despite being strenuous, this is perhaps the most popular hike on the west side of the Tetons. There are good reasons for this. One is a magnificent payoff at the top. When you scramble those last few yards, you are treated to a view of all the range's big peaks. This hike is also popular because it can give novices a real sense of accomplishment. The trail can be crowded throughout July when area Boy Scout and girls' summer camps send groups up the mountain.

As with any tough hikes, you'll enjoy this one if you are in good condition.

There are two routes up the mountain. The longer, more gradual main route — sometimes called "The Huckleberry Trail" and the shorter ridge trail.

The ridge route trims at least an hour and a half of hiking off the main route, but it is steep and not recommended under wet or slippery conditions. It is usually the route taken during winter ascents.

To access the ridge route, drive to the South Teton Creek trailhead as if you're going to hike to Alaska Basin. Look for a small trail on the northside of the restroom. This is the ridge trail. Most of the hike's elevation gain comes in the first 2.5 miles. As you gain the top of the canyon, you'll be treated to some nice views of the South Fork Teton canyon. After 2.5 miles, you gain the main ridge leading up to Table Mountain. At three miles, the trail joins the main trail up to the summit block.

The main "Huckleberry" trail follows the North Fork of Teton Creek. To access this trail, park at the trailhead before you cross the creek bridge near the campground. The hike starts out with switchbacks for the first .5 miles until you climb about four hundred feet. After this first initial workout, the trail settles in for a

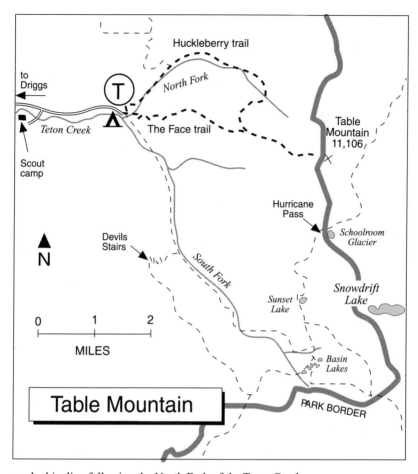

The Face trail

Huckleberry trail

North Fork

to Driggs

T

Teton Creek

Scout camp

N

Devils Stairs

South Fork

Table Mountain 11,106

Hurricane Pass

Schoolroom Glacier

Snowdrift Lake

Sunset Lake

Basin Lakes

0   1   2
MILES

Table Mountain

PARK BORDER

gradual incline following the North Fork of the Teton Creek.

After a few hundred yards, the trail enters the Jedediah Smith Wilderness Area. The Forest Service has limited the maximum number of people in each group on the trails. Check for current regulations. Wildflowers are usually in abundance along this trail during mid-July and early August. Moose are sometimes seen in the willows near the creek.

The trail crosses the creek three times before it begins to climb abruptly again. At about the 3.5-mile mark, the trail begins to switchback up to the mountain's summit ridge. This ridge is at the 9,900-foot level. As you climb to this ridge, the trail enters into the alpine tundra zone. Here, summer is short and few trees survive. Those that are alive are stunted, bent and twisted. You often encounter snowfields across the trail.

Once you are at the top of the ridge, the thin air and lack of barriers to sight play tricks on your perception. It looks like Table Mountain is just up ahead, but in fact you've still got two miles to go and more than 1,000 feet of elevation to gain.

The last mile can be tough on tired legs. Be patient, rest often, snack and drink regularly.

The last hundred yards is a scramble up to the box-shaped summit block and then comes the wonderful reward. The view is breathtaking — and not just because you're out of breath. Remember to pack a camera and/or binoculars. From this vantage point there is so much to see. It's a good place to linger and eat lunch. The flat-topped mountain summit is about as long and wide as a couple of school buses set next to each other. With a pair of binoculars you can pick out climbers picking their way to the top of the Grand Teton just to the east.

FOSSIL MOUNTAIN

GETTING THERE: From Victor, Idaho, drive 5.5 miles north on Highway 33. Turn right (east) onto a paved road. Look for signs at the beginning of the road for Darby Girls Camp. After a mile the road becomes gravel. After another half mile the road forks. Go right and follow this road about 6 miles to its end, where you may park.

DISTANCE: About 6 miles to the top.

DIFFICULTY: Moderately strenuous.

SEASON: July to October.

SPECIAL CONSIDERATIONS: Expect to see tons of fossils on the side of the summit block.

The easiest way to the top of 10,916-foot Fossil Mountain is up the South Fork of Darby Canyon trail. Most people know of this trail as the Wind Cave trail or (in girls camp circles) the Monument Trail. Because of the nearby Darby Girls Camp, this trail probably gets as much use on some weekdays as it does on weekends.

The trail begins at the end of the Darby Canyon road and crosses the creek on a footbridge. After about a half mile, the trail enters the Jedediah Smith Wilderness Area. From here it gently switchbacks up the South Fork of Darby Canyon.

In midsummer this canyon is filled with wild flowers.

After about 3 miles, the trail crosses to the west side of the canyon and heads for the Wind Cave. There is a faint trail that continues up the canyon toward Fossil Mountain.

The faint trail soon fades away. Don't worry about getting off track. Just set your sights on the pass to the southwest of Fossil Mountain and hike the path of least resistance.

When Fossil Mountain appears in view, its west face is imposing. It's almost straight up, cliffy and loose rock.

Two miles after leaving the main trail, you'll reach the Fossil Mountain pass.

From the pass, there is a faint trail that starts up the ridge to Fossil Mountain. The peak's south end is a steep ramp of broken and loose rock. The hiking up is slow, but not too hard.

Almost at every turn, ancient seabed creatures — clams, coral, seaweed — lie cemented into the broken up rock. There are also geode crystals broken open and on display. What might be an uneventful grunt up the side of a mountain becomes a slog of discovery.

After about a third of a mile, the ramp of scree gives way to the level summit ridge. A few hundred feet north and you're standing next to a cairn with a summit

36

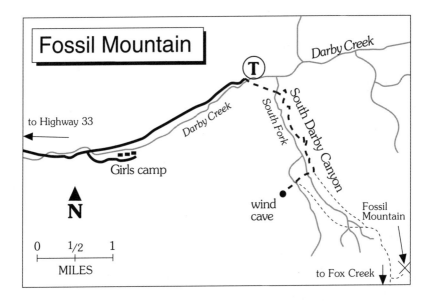

register inside.

The views from the top of Fossil Mountain take in the southern end of the Tetons. You can easily make out the tram on the top of Rendezvous Peak. To the southeast, you can see the tops of the Wind River Range.

Coming down from the mountain can be more taxing than going up. The loose rock occasionally will scoot out from under and bite legs and hands.

On warm summer days, beat the heat by detouring to the Wind Cave on the way back down the canyon. The cave is like a giant, frosty air conditioned room.

BALDY PEAK

GETTING THERE: Drive southeast from Swan Valley on U.S. Highway 26 to Irwin. Turn left on the Palisades Creek Road at the sign for Palisades Creek Campground. Follow this road for 1.5 miles. Just before the campground and a bridge across the creek is a parking area. Park here.

DISTANCE: About 3 miles round-trip.

DIFFICULTY: Strenuous.

SEASON: April and May for skiing/snowboarding. June to November for hiking. Go early in the morning to beat the afternoon heat.

SPECIAL CONSIDERATIONS: The large summit-to-base gully facing Swan Valley avalanches in late winter/early spring (often in April) — don't be around when it happens. Skiing is safest after the avalanche occurs.

Don't let Baldy Peak in the Snake River Mountains fool you. Although it looks like a doddering old grandpa of a mountain with bald top and mellow-looking ridges, it takes a bit of muscle and determination to bag this peak.

With a 4,000-foot elevation gain and steep snow-drifted ridges, this climb can

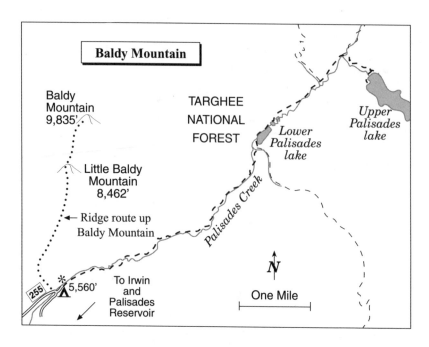

Baldy Mountain

Baldy
Mountain
9,835'

TARGHEE
NATIONAL
FOREST

Upper
Palisades
lake

Lower
Palisades
lake

Little Baldy
Mountain
8,462'

← Ridge route up
Baldy Mountain

Palisades Creek

255

▲5,560'

To Irwin
and
Palisades
Reservoir

N

One Mile

be a rewarding conditioner. The peak appeals to more than just peak baggers seeking nice views overlooking Palisades Reservoir and the Snake River valley. Backcountry skiers and snowboarders often climb the peak in late winter and spring to test their mettle on the long southwest gully or south-facing bowl just below the

Summit register on Baldy Peak is an ammunition canister wired to a post.

A herd of mountain goats hang out on the steep slopes of Baldy Mountain.

summit.

There are two popular routes up Baldy Peak: The long and mellow route from the Rainey Creek trail and the short and grinding ridge from the Palisades Creek trail parking area.

Most prefer the short route. From the parking lot at Palisades Creek trail, scramble up to the ridge on the other side of the fence that marks the forest boundary. This ridge is the one on your left if you are facing upstream, up the Palisades Creek Canyon.

The steep slog begins immediately. The elevation is about 5,600 feet at the car and 9,835 feet at the summit. The 4,000 feet of vertical are gained in less than 3 miles. Once on the ridge, the climb is fairly straightforward. Stay on the ridge and it will take you all the way to the top. It helps if the day is clear enough to see the summit in the distance.

The ridge is not all uphill, though. About a third of the way up the ridge is a high spot called Little Baldy. There is a waist-high cairn marking the spot. In this area, there are resident moose. Look for moose sign along the ridge for the next half-mile. Also keep your eyes open for mountain goats on the open slopes.

From Little Baldy, the ridge dips slightly before climbing steeply up to some rocky high points. When in doubt, stay as close to the ridgeline as possible.

About two-thirds of the way up, the ridge levels one last time before making a final steep ascent to the summit.

The final 200 to 300 yards are steep and loose.

The summit has an old military ammunition can with notes of people who have climbed the peak. On clear days, you'll spot the Tetons to the northeast and the mountains of central Idaho to the west.

Unless you're strapped into skis or a snowboard, the descent off Baldy is a mixed blessing. What took hours to climb, takes only minutes to plunge/ski or hike down. On the downside, your quad muscles pay a price for all that quick descending. It's a good idea to stop every 15 minutes or so and relax.

SHEEP CREEK PEAK

GETTING THERE: From Swan Valley, drive southeast on Highway 26 about 10 miles. About 3/4 mile south of the Gaging Station turn left (north) onto Sheep Creek Road. There is a sign for the road, but it can't be read when heading southeast. Drive 2 miles up Sheep Creek Road. Near the sign for the Mennonite Camp, the road forks. Keep right. The road gets rutted and bumpy for the next mile. The trailhead is at a Forest Service sign next to the road.

This is a trail with quick payoffs and rewards.

The rewards for climbing Sheep Creek Peak (try to say that fast three or four times) are a stunning view of eastern Idaho and western Wyoming and the chance to see mountain goats and other wildlife.

Another benefit of hiking this trail is the solitude. While most of eastern Idaho's hikers will be one canyon north of you hiking the Palisades Creek Trail, you'll likely have the Sheep Creek Peak Trail all to yourself.

Sheep Creek Peak, 9,950 feet, is one of those giants you see along the highway as you drive to Palisades Reservoir. The peak is one of a trio of large peaks on the northeast side of the reservoir near the dam. The other two giants are Mount Baird, at 10,025 feet and Elkhorn Peak, at 9,940 feet.

There are two main ways to get to the top of Sheep Creek Peak. The first, and shortest, is to hike up the Sheep Creek Trail. This trail connects into the Waterfall Canyon Trail and is one of the shortest ways to get to the waterfalls — but not necessarily the easiest.

The other approach to Sheep Creek Peak is from the Little Elk Creek Trail. In early summer, the Little Elk Creek approach often has much more snow.

The trail starts at the end of the bumpy Sheep Creek Road. A high-clearance vehicle is recommended for the last half-mile. The road ends at a Forest Service sign which names the trail and says "Waterfall Can. 4." About 3/4 of a mile up the

Fresh mountain goat tracks are seen in the snow just below Sheep Creek Peak.

trail another Forest Service sign says "Waterfall Can. 5." Five miles is about right from the trailhead to the top of Waterfall Canyon.

The top of Sheep Creek Peak is about 3.5 miles from the end of the road.

The trail starts out as an old jeep road and slowly narrows into an ATV type trail. The trail becomes a footpath after a little more than a half mile. Elevation gain is a steady uphill almost the entire way. From the trailhead to the base of the peak, the trail gains about 3,000 feet.

One thing to keep in mind is that the Sheep Creek Canyon doesn't have much water in it. Once the snow has melted, the canyon will be dry, especially up high. Bring all your water for day and overnight trips.

After about two miles, the canyon narrows and becomes even steeper.

In early July, the upper parts of the canyon are still covered with large snow patches. In some places, the trail disappears under snow. But you shouldn't get lost if you stick to the main canyon.

At the top of the canyon the trail enters a small basin. Here hikers are treated to the view of the long, crescent-shaped ridge of Sheep Creek Peak. The summit is still about 500 to 600 feet above. Look for mountain goats cooling themselves on lingering snow patches along the summit ridge.

From the base of the ridge there are different ways to the top. The main idea is to get on the summit ridge, then walk it to the summit.

Two good routes to the summit ridge include switchbacking up a low point along the northwest ridge or scrambling up a prominent rocky rib on the northern face.

As soon as you hit the summit ridge, you are treated to one of the best views in the entire Palisades area. All of the reservoir, the north end of the Salt River Range, the Gros Ventre Range, the upper end of the Wind River Range, the Tetons, the Centennial Range and more suddenly jump into view. It's worth doing again for that view.

On the summit is a small cairn. Tucked inside is a small register.

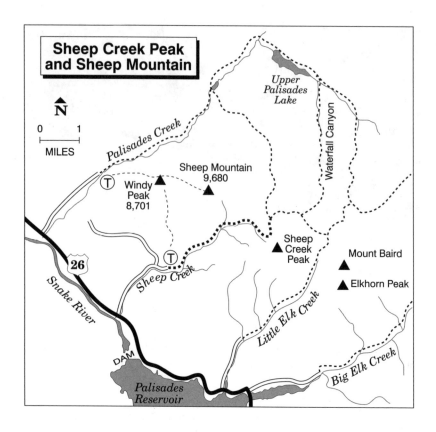

Sheep Creek Peak
and Sheep Mountain

N

0   1

MILES

Palisades Creek

Upper
Palisades
Lake

Waterfall Canyon

Sheep Mountain
9,680

Windy
Peak
8,701

Sheep Creek

Sheep
Creek
Peak

Mount Baird

Elkhorn Peak

26

Snake River

Little Elk Creek

DAM

Palisades
Reservoir

Big Elk Creek

SHEEP MOUNTAIN

GETTING THERE: See text.
DISTANCE: About 3.5 miles one-way.
DIFFICULTY: Strenuous, gains about 4,500 feet.
SPECIAL CONSIDERATIONS: Keep your eyes open for mountain goats. They are often seen below the cliffs near the summit. Bring along binoculars.

The fun of climbing this mountain is the awesome views from the top.

On a clear day, you'll be treated to some nice views of the surrounding Snake River mountains, the Greys River Range to the south and the Tetons to the northeast. Below you is the Snake River valley and the blue waters of Palisades Reservoir.

There are two different main routes to the top of Sheep Mountain. Either route requires some serious uphill hiking.

Route 1: Park at the Palisades Creek trailhead, walk over the bridge and hike to the base of the southeast side of Palisades Creek canyon. Follow a barbed wire fence up the canyon rim for about a quarter of a mile. This route basically climbs and follows the Palisades Creek canyon rim.

The first high point is called Windy Peak (8,701) on the Targhee Forest Service maps. It can be a bit disheartening knowing that you have another mile and another 1,000 feet up to go from here. Stick with it, though, the top is awesome. Follow the ridgeline which turns and heads almost straight east. It's a good idea to occasionally look back the way you have come so that you can find your way back. Some of the side ridges could fool you on the way down.

The final summit push is steep until you arrive on the summit ridge.

One odd thing on this hike is patches of cactus. Look for mountain goats in the large rocky bowl between Sheep Mountain and Windy Peak.

Route 2: This route starts by driving up the road to the Sheep Creek summer home area just before the Palisades Dam. About two miles up the road take a left up Sawmill Canyon. The road ends after a mile or so depending on your vehicle.

From the end of the poor road, you will be about 1.5 miles (as the crow flies) southwest from Windy Peak. Climb the ridge next to the canyon (called Canary Canyon on the Targhee Forest Service map) and go up toward Windy Peak. From the top of Windy Peak, follow the ridgeline to Sheep Mountain.

Remember to save some energy for the return trip. As with most mountains, going down can be a quad-burner.

ELK MOUNTAIN LOOKOUT

DISTANCE: 5 miles roundtrip.
DIFFICULTY: Strenuous.
GETTING THERE: See text.

Just south of Alpine, Wyo., is a beautiful canyon that boasts several trailheads, primitive campsites, a lively river and abundant wildlife.

The Greys River Road leads right out of the town of Alpine and within minutes you'll find yourself in the backcountry. Among the several fun trails is a lookout high on the Elk Mountain ridge. This area is sometimes called the Greys River Range, but it is all part of the Wyoming Range that runs north and south for more than 50 miles south of Hoback, Wyo., and east of Star Valley. The range is separated from the Tetons to the north by the Snake River canyon and boasts several 10,000 footers.

In the fall, half the fun is driving the winding road along the east side of the Palisades Reservoir. The aspens are a bright yellow and present a picture perfect setting. The drive up the Greys River Canyon is just as beautiful.

Few of the trailheads are marked with signs. To find the trail to the lookout, drive a few miles up the Greys River Road to an intersection with the Little Greys River. Turn left and drive 1.2 miles up this road and turn left on a narrow dirt road. Drive about a quarter of a mile or until the road gets too bumpy for your liking. The road quickly degenerates into an ATV trail after the last campsite.

The Bridger-Teton Forest Service map calls this trail "Trail Creek." It starts out as a mellow ATV trail and gets steeper and steeper. There are a few side trails created by grazing cattle that could possibly confuse hikers. The main idea is to stick to the main route and keep right to climb up to a ridgetop after about two miles. If the trail you are hiking drops down, you're probably off track.

Clouds swirl around the Elk Mountain Lookout in the Wyoming Range.

After two miles of uphill, the trail connects with a ridge. Follow the ridge, which will hook south. Eventually, if you sight along the ridge to the south, you will see a small building in the distance. The trail sticks to the ridgeline and takes you to this lookout.

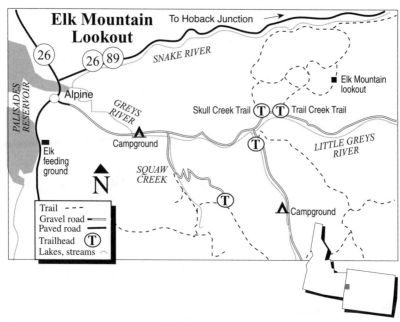

While not the most picturesque of buildings, this small, one-room lookout does get you out of the wind, and it provides a 360-degree panoramic view of most of the range.

Inside the lookout are goofy notes and names scratched and penciled on the walls. Some (if you can believe the dates) are almost 40 years old.

The building has been repaired in recent years. Some of the broken glass panes have been replaced with Plexiglas.

One of the nice things about the view is that it inspires you to explore more canyons and ridges in the Wyoming Range. You can access some of these areas for backcountry skiing. Allow extra time and energy to ski up to the mountains because most of the roads are not plowed in winter, or you can hitch a ride on a snowmobile to reach the slopes. A good source of information on some of the peaks in this area is Tom Turiano's encyclopedic "Select Peaks of Greater Yellowstone."

MOUNT McCALEB

GETTING THERE: From Arco, drive north on Highway 93 about 20 miles to the town of Mackay. Turn right on Main Street and follow the road 1.9 miles and turn left on Lower Cedar Creek Road. Follow this road to near the end at the mouth of the canyon (stay above the creek ravine). About a quarter of a mile before the mouth of the canyon, take a jeep road to the left that heads to the northwest and

A deer trots past the scree fields several hundred feet below the summit block of Mount McCaleb in the Lost River Range.

45

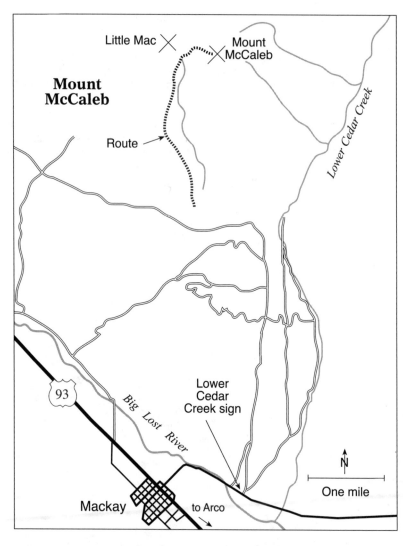

angles toward the mountain. Drive as close to the foot of the mountain as your vehicle will take you. Pass two jeep roads and take the third if you are driving a high-clearance vehicle with power. There is a very steep jeep trail up the side of the mountain that is only recommended for ATV or powerful four-wheel drive machines. From your parking spot, hike up the prominent gulley between Little Mac and Mount McCaleb. For more information and photos, go to www.idaho-summits.com.

DISTANCE: 6 to 9 miles roundtrip depending on how close you can drive to the mountain.

DIFFICULTY: Very strenuous. Gains nearly 5,000 feet in elevation.

Mount McCaleb, at 11,600+ feet, is that picturesque peak to the east of Mackay. It's one of the last of the big brutes on the southern end of the Lost River Range. Like many of the peaks in the range, the top has a huge vertical cliff face – perhaps 300 feet high — that gives the impression that only serious climbers need apply. Fortunately the west ridge of the peak offers a straightforward – albeit, arduous – "dog route" to the summit.

One of the hardest parts about climbing this peak is getting to the base of the mountain. The Lower Cedar Creek Road is accessible with a sedan and careful driving, but a high-clearance vehicle is preferred. You can park near the mouth of the Lower Cedar Creek Canyon and hike northwest along the base of the mountain. With a high-clearance vehicle and the extra time to explore the maze of jeep trails, it is possible to drive closer to the route. If you park at the mouth of Lower Cedar Creek canyon, add about two miles (one way) to the hike.

The trick to finding the easiest route up McCaleb is picking the right starting ridge. It's easy to see from the highway near Mackay, but harder once you drive and hike to the base of the mountain. There is an intermitent trail up the ridge that puts you onto the northwest side of the peak. When you pop out of the treeline, you are staring at the huge slope of loose scree. Be forewarned that the top looks closer than it really is. From the treeline to the summit is more than 1,000 feet of elevation gain.

You can hike up an obvious gully that leads to the west ridge or go straight up the southwest line and work around to the west face. Snow often lingers on this face throughout the year.

The summit of Mount McCaleb is a narrow strip that drops off abruptly on the east, south and north sides. There are technical routes up the southwest cliffs of McCaleb in the 5.7 to 5.10 difficulty range.

NOTE: If this peak whets your appetite for more exploring and peak-bagging in the Lost River Range, refer to the book "Trails of Eastern Idaho" by Margaret Fuller and Jerry Painter for a guide to all of Idaho's 12,000-foot peaks.

Biking

HARRIMAN STATE PARK

GETTING THERE: From Ashton, Idaho, drive north on Highway 20 about 20 miles. The turnoff for the park is before you come to State Road 47. The park headquarters are about .5 miles from the highway. A per-vehicle entrance fee is charged.

Harriman State Park, often considered a fisherman's haven in the summer and

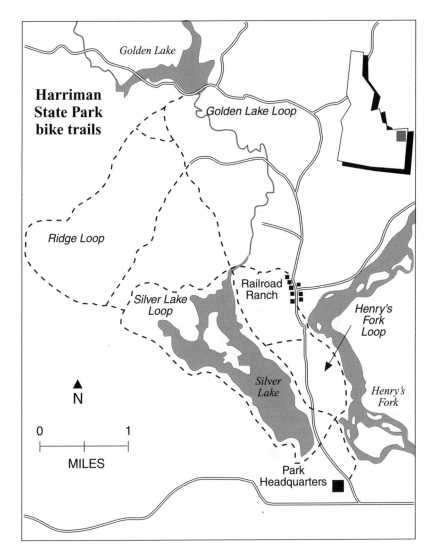

Harriman
State Park
bike trails

Golden Lake

Golden Lake Loop

Ridge Loop

Railroad
Ranch

Silver Lake
Loop

Henry's
Fork
Loop

Silver
Lake

Henry's
Fork

N

0   1
|----+----|
   MILES

Park
Headquarters

a skier's destination in the winter, offers a little something for most riders. If you've been there in the winter to ski, than you're already familiar with the trail system.

While most of the trails are considered mellow biking, you can get some big ups and downs by heading up Thurmon Ridge and you can get some distance by riding along the river to Island Park Reservoir Dam or by adding extra loops on the trails.

These trails are shared by hikers and horseback riders, but most weekends traffic is minimal. If you're worried about crowds, check at the main office to see which trails are most likely to be packed.

If you've only been to the park in the winter, Harriman can be a treat in the summer. Perhaps the most popular — and scenic — routes are the trails that follow the Henry's Fork River and the loop around Silver Lake. These routes also offer some tree cover to avoid the summer sun. The route out to Golden Lake is less forested.

Because the trails are maintained for skiers and horseback riders, they are also accommodating of bikers. The only trail you may have to duck and dodge tree limbs on is the Thurmon Ridge trail.

The lower trails are mostly flat and easy to ride. It's a good place to bring children and novice riders.

Just like hiking, it pays to get out of bed early to avoid the heat and possible thunderstorms of the summer afternoons.

OLD RAILROAD TRAIL

MAPS: Targhee National Forest

GETTING THERE: There are several trailheads for the trail. If you want to do the whole trail, probably the best place to start is at Reas Pass, so your trip will be all downhill. Although the railroad bed exists from Reas Pass to West Yellowstone, following the trail can be confusing. To begin at Reas Pass, drive on U.S. Highway 20 to a point 2 miles west of West Yellowstone. Here turn south onto the South Fork of the Madison River Road. Passenger cars can drive to Reas Pass, which is about 7 miles from the highway.

Another trailhead is at the Black Canyon Road east of Mack's Inn. To reach it, take U.S. Highway 20 to Mack's Inn, about 33 miles north of Ashton. Turn east at Mack's Inn on Forest Road 059 and follow the signs to Big Springs. At Big Springs, turn north on the Black Canyon Road (Forest Road 066) and drive 6 miles. A sign marks where the road intersects the rail trail. There is parking along the road just before the intersection. From here, you can go to Reas Pass or start south toward Warm River.

The Warm River Campground is at the south end of the trail. To reach it, drive east of Ashton on Idaho Highway 47 and go north on Mesa Falls Road for about 10 miles, following the signs for Warm River.

For more details and a map on this and other hiking and biking trails, consult the guidebook "Trails of Eastern Idaho" by Jerry Painter and Margaret Fuller. The book on more than 100 area trails is available at area bookstores and sporting goods stores.

This trail goes by several names. The old railroad bed trail from Reas Pass to Warm River is considered by many to be one of the best long mountain biking routes in eastern Idaho, and one of the best in the state. The trail follows the old Yellowstone Special route, which carried tourists from Pocatello and Idaho Falls to Yellowstone National Park's West Entrance during the first half of the century. The old steam engines chugged through the farmland and backcountry for decades until the line was no longer financially sustainable. When the tracks were torn out, the trail that remained was graded, and trestle bridges were refurbished for horseback riders and mountain bikers in summer and snowmobilers in the winter.

Today, the trail is so good that it's like riding a soft sidewalk though the back-

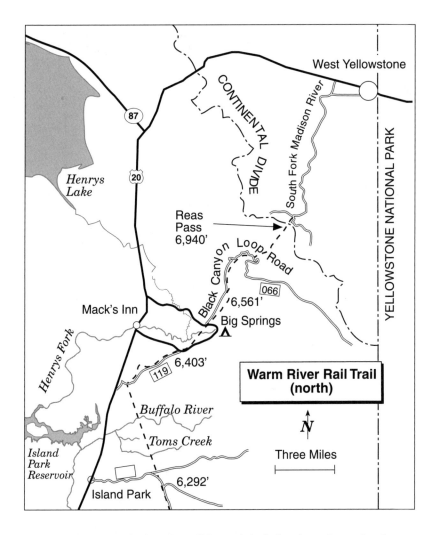

West Yellowstone

CONTINENTAL DIVIDE

South Fork Madison River

YELLOWSTONE NATIONAL PARK

Henrys Lake

87

20

Reas Pass 6,940'

Black Canyon Loop Road

066

6,561'

Mack's Inn

Big Springs

Λ

Henrys Fork

119   6,403'

Warm River Rail Trail (north)

Buffalo River

Toms Creek

N

Three Miles

Island Park Reservoir

Island Park

6,292'

country. About the only time the trail is rough is during the spring and early summer. During this time, trail users face downed trees across the trail and occasional boggy areas that often flood the trail. By midsummer, most of the water has receded and the downfall has been cleared away.

Because the trail is a railroad grade and gains elevation slowly, it's a great beginner route or a good long-distance trip for those in good shape. The nice thing about this trail is that it's interesting. Just about the time you tire of the endless sea of lodgepole pines, the trail crosses a trestle bridge over a creek, or the forest opens up to reveal a gorgeous view of the Island Park plateau. Places such as Big Springs, Buffalo River and Warm River offer great opportunities for side trips, especially if you want to stop and camp and do some fishing.

Because the route is intersected by side roads, it's easy to break the trail into

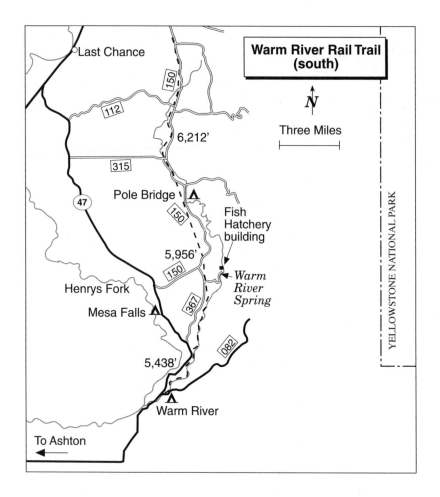

shorter sections. This works well if you have children along or if you want to do the entire route over a few weekends.

The entire route is about 48 miles long (add another 10 miles if you start from West Yellowstone), which means car shuttles have to be creative. You can start at the intersection of the Black Canyon Road with the trail, or start at Reas Pass on the Idaho-Montana border. The section from Reas Pass to Black Canyon is the toughest part of the whole trail, but experienced mountain bikers will find it pretty easy.

The section from Reas Pass to the Black Canyon Road is part of the Continental Divide Trail. It is 2.5 miles from the Black Canyon Road to Reas Pass.

Continuing south from the Black Canyon Road, the first five miles until Big Springs are scenic. The trail passes though thick forest and deep canyons. A couple of vistas open up, allowing you to see most of the upper end of the Island Park plateau. There is also a glimpse of the distant Teton range. The route descends quickly out of the Henry's Lake Mountains down to the plateau.

Big Springs is a nice side trip for those with some extra time. The springs provide most of the flow for the Henry's Fork of the Snake River until it is joined by the Buffalo River.

Just beyond the springs the trail crosses the Henry's Fork on a long trestle bridge.

A mile past Buffalo River the trail passes through a huge meadow of several square miles.

One highlight, especially for kids, is the railroad tunnel. About three miles out from the Warm River Campground the trail passes though a tunnel in the rock. It is long enough to become fairly dark inside.

The Warm River Campground is the end of the line. Here, paved roads take over the old railroad grade. The trail comes in at the upper end of the campground. There is plenty of parking outside the campground and several nice campsites with restrooms and tables in the campground.

CITY CREEK

DIRECTIONS: See map page 54.

The City Creek Trail is a fun half-day trip right out of Pocatello into the nearby foothills. This trail attracts hikers and mountain bikers throughout the spring, summer and fall.

This trail can get a lot of use, especially on weekends, so an early start can be helpful in avoiding the traffic.

City Creek flows northeast and enters town on the southeast side before joining the Portneuf River. The creek is small and shallow but runs year-round except in severe drought years. It can be jumped in most places.

From Grant Avenue, the trail starts out paralleling the south (left) side of the creek and heads up the draw.

Unlike many mountain streams, City Creek doesn't pass through a deep wooded canyon. Instead it flows through a shallow draw. Along the draw is a thick ribbon of maples, aspens and willows. Outside the draw it is practically barren, with only grasses and brush growing on the hillsides.

The trail is mostly a gentle up and down, but it has a steady uphill gain. After the first mile, the trail comes out onto a dirt road. Follow the dirt road about 100 yards. Take the footbridge on your left and re-enter the ribbon of forest on the single-track trail. You can also cut southeast to Cusick Creek to make a fun loop trip.

The potential for head-on collisions with other users is great on this trail. Some sections offer short visibility and blind corners. Be especially cautious when riding downhill and make noise on blind corners.

MINK CREEK AREA

GETTING THERE: From Pocatello, drive south on Interstate 15 10 miles and take the exit to Portneuf. Follow the signs to Mink Creek Recreation Area. Drive 5 miles from Portneuf south up the Bannock Highway to Cherry Springs Natural Area. Drive 2 miles south of Cherry Springs and turn left (east) and follow the signs to Scout Mountain Campground and Crestline Trailhead. Drive 4 miles south

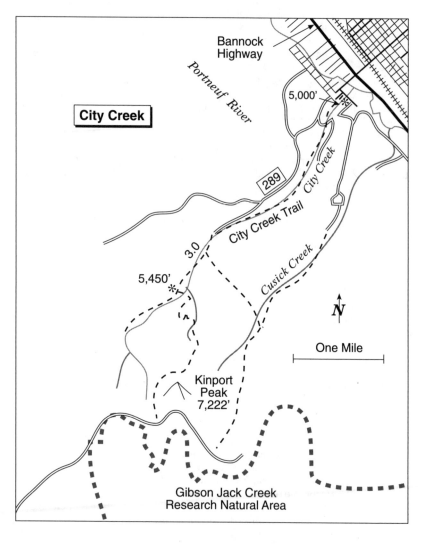

City Creek

Bannock Highway

Portneuf River

5,000'

289

City Creek Trail

City Creek

Cusick Creek

3.0

5,450'

N

One Mile

Kinport Peak 7,222'

Gibson Jack Creek Research Natural Area

on Bannock Highway from Cherry Springs to the Valve House Draw and West Mink Creek trailheads. West Mink Creek is on the west side of the road about 50 yards south from the Valve House Draw trailhead which is on the east side. There is no sign that says, West Mink Creek. There is a small Forest Service sign with the number 059. Valve House Draw has a large gate at the trailhead. Its Forest Service number is 5171.

HOW STRENUOUS: West Mink Creek and Valve House Draw are moderate to strenuous depending on your distance. Scout Mountain Campground loop to Crestline is strenuous.

ELEVATIONS: West Mink Creek and Valve House Draw both start out at

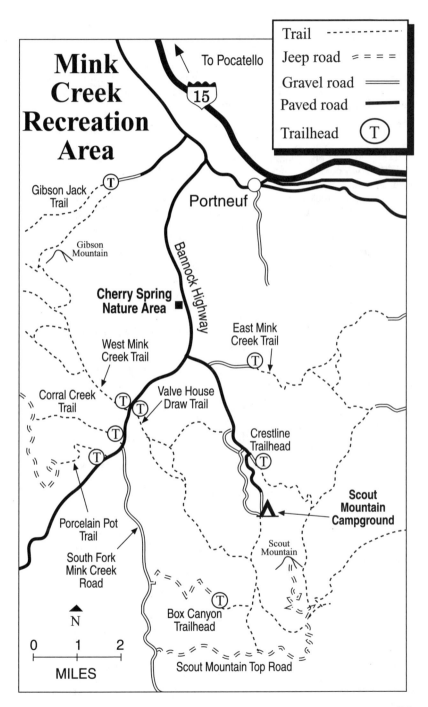

Mink Creek Recreation Area

Trail `----------`
Jeep road `= = = =`
Gravel road `=====`
Paved road `━━━`
Trailhead Ⓣ

To Pocatello

15

Gibson Jack Trail Ⓣ

Portneuf

Gibson Mountain

Cherry Spring Nature Area ■

Bannock Highway

East Mink Creek Trail Ⓣ

West Mink Creek Trail

Corral Creek Trail Ⓣ Ⓣ

Valve House Draw Trail Ⓣ

Ⓣ

Ⓣ

Crestline Trailhead Ⓣ

Scout Mountain Campground

Porcelain Pot Trail

South Fork Mink Creek Road

Scout Mountain

N

0 1 2
MILES

Box Canyon Trailhead Ⓣ

Scout Mountain Top Road

55

5,200 feet and top out at 6,600 feet. Scout Mountain Campground is at 6,500 feet and climbs to 8,350 and back down to 6,000 at the Crestline Trailhead. Add another 700 feet if you take the side trip to the top of Scout Mountain.

DISTANCES: The Scout Mountain Campground to Crestline Trailhead is 13.5 miles. Add 4 miles if you go to the top of Scout Mountain. West Mink Creek to its junction with Gibson Jack is 6 miles. Valve Spring Draw to its junction with the trail south of Scout Mountain is 7.5 miles.

The Mink Creek area is popular with bikers because most of the trails are open to mountain bikes at least part of the year. To help prevent erosion, many of the trails are closed to biking during the winter months. Most open March 15 and close Dec. 30. Two popular, moderately easy trails are West Mink Creek and Valve House Draw.

West Mink Creek trail follows the creek up a canyon forested with fir and aspen. Good foot bridges take care of the three stream crossings. The springs at the upper end of the watershed are used for municipal water. Because of this, dogs are not allowed on this trail. Most of the trail is also a "research natural area." This designation boils down to no motorized vehicles of any kind allowed and no camping. If you want to camp, you'll have to do so outside of the "natural area."

The Valve House Draw trail just north of West Mink Creek is open to hikers, horses, mountain bikers, motorcycles and ATVs that meet certain size restrictions. The first part of the trail was once a jeep trail. The trail follows a spring-fed creek for about 6 miles. After 8 miles the trail joins the trail that goes south out of Scout Mountain Campground. This trail allows dogs, but doesn't open for bike use until mid March. Camping is permitted. The canyon is mostly forested and offers some nice views.

Bikers looking for a loop route can ride south on the South Fork Mink Creek Road and turn east up Box Canyon and continue on until you connect with the trail coming south from Scout Mountain Campground. Head north on this trail until you connect with the Valve House Draw trail. Complete the loop by riding the 1.5 miles back to South Fork Mink Creek Road on the paved Bannock Highway. This loop has the advantage of a mostly gradual climb up Box Canyon and mostly downhill on the Valve House Draw trail.

Bikers looking for a serious workout can take on the Scout Mountain to Crestline loop. Start at the Scout Mountain Campground near the nature trail. The trail heads due south for 2 miles then turns east and circles around the south side of Scout Mountain and starts heading north when you reach a junction with a jeep trail. This jeep trail offers a steep side trip up to the top of Scout Mountain. Add an extra 4 miles to the trip if you wind your way up to the top of the mountain. The trail leaves the jeep trail after .5 miles and heads due north 2.5 miles along a ridge. You will come to a junction. Take the left fork and switchback down two miles to the Crestline trailhead. This 13-mile loop gains and loses close to 2,000 feet.

KELLY CANYON AREA

GETTING THERE: From Idaho Falls drive east on Highway 26 for about 16 miles and turn left at the signs for Kelly Canyon Ski Hill and Heise Hot Springs – continue following the signs to the ski hill. At 3 miles, turn right after crossing the

Snake River and continue past the hot springs, past the golf course on your right and continue all the way up to Kelly Canyon Ski Hill. The listed trails have individual directions from the ski hill.

Buckskin Morgan Ridge/ Fenceline/Hawley Gulch Loop

From the ski hill, continue driving on the gravel road for about 1 mile and park at the "Y-junction" where the road splits 3 ways. The ride starts up the left fork in the road (FR 218), and ascends switchbacks before topping out on Morgan Summit at about .9 miles. The Buckskin trail starts from here off the left side of the road.

Follow the single track as it climbs a short, steep section before leveling out for a fantastic ride that winds through the forested ridgeline. At 2.6 miles the single track ends and merges with a 2-track road. Take a hard right and follow the 2-track as it dips, climbs and winds its way along the forested ridge. The dirt gives way to a rocky two-track as it crests and drops for a fantastic descent with two hairpin corners. At about 4.8 miles try not to miss a remnant of a road on the left. Take this turn and climb briefly before dropping down on a faded track – there is a fenceline on the right that parallels the trail as it climbs gently again through the trees before dropping down and through a gate at 5.4 miles. Pass through the gate and take a right. At 5.45 miles make a right on an old road that has "tank traps" and usually stagnant pond-like water in it. Pass the traps and open it up on the descent as the road gives way to a single track with a stout little kicker near the end. Ride or step through the small creek and join up with FR 218 at 6.08 miles. Make a right and head up the road passing over a cattle guard and at 6.3 miles take the faint trail on the left. Ascend through thick growth, descend, make a left and head for the two-track at 6.46 miles. From here go right and at 6.66 miles make another right onto a single track. Follow this as it weaves its way through the forest and drops steeply and merges with another single track at 6.95 miles, from here make a left. At 7.23 miles cross a bridge over Hawley Creek and climb the short steep hillside to connect with a dirt road. Follow this road downstream as it gives way to a single track before merging with the old Haw-

Steve Fischbach rides the Buckskin-Morgan Ridge trail at Kelly Canyon.

57

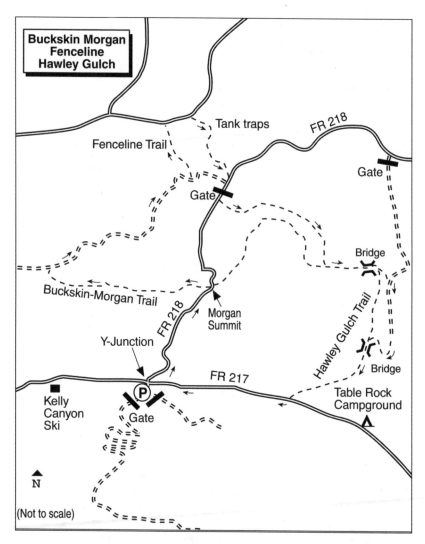

ley Gulch trail and bridge at 8.3 miles. Navigate the loose scree and pass the Poison Flats trail before enjoying the descent into Table Rock Campground. CAUTION: Please be courteous of uphill travel through this section of trail. This portion of the trail sees heavy use during the weekends. Connect with FR 217 at 9.12 miles and take a right climbing the road back to the parking area at about 10.4 miles.

Hawley Gulch/Wolverine Creek Loop

An all-time favorite, Wolverine Creek ranks the highest with local bikers who have ridden here for years. This trail is most enjoyable as a downhill/loop ride but

Cranking along the Wolverine Creek trail at Kelly Canyon.

hard-core cyclists are known to do it as an up-and-back. From the ski hill, drive up the gravel road to the "Y-junction" and take the middle fork in the road that descends to Table Rock Campground; park here.

Peddle from the campground back up the dirt road and take a right at about .52 miles into the Poison Flats parking area. Ride through the loose gravel and start up the wide trail. Follow the single track as it weaves its way through the trees and eventually joins up with the Hawley Gulch trail at .96 miles. Turn left onto the Hawley Gulch trail and continue climbing upstream. Turn right at the foot bridge and peddle up the short switchbacks. Continue on the wide flat trail as it passes over a cattle guard, takes a sharp left and flattens out again before joining FR218 at 2.64 miles. From here turn right and follow the main dirt road as it climbs briefly, then flattens out before climbing again to top out on Windy Ridge. From here it's mostly downhill! As the road descends, look to the right at about 4.46 miles for road 883; take this two-track. Where the two-track/road takes a sharp left, drop down off the track angling left and look for the start of another less defined two-track. Follow the trail as it descends through the trees and switchbacks before opening up in a flat meadow. Climb up a short incline before descending again and passing through Wolverine Creek and the final section before the trail empties out on the river road at about 9.39 miles. Turn right and follow the road as it climbs back up to Table Rock Campground at 13.10 miles.

Stinking Springs

If you like long climbs that are rewarded with steep and technical downhills

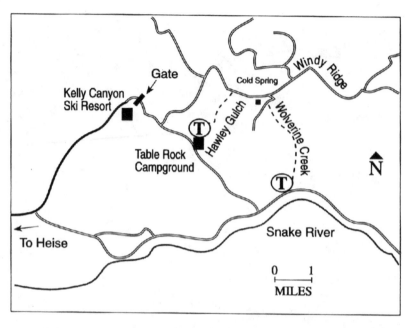

Map labels:

Gate

Kelly Canyon Ski Resort

Cold Spring

Windy Ridge

T

Hawley Gulch

Wolverine Creek

Table Rock Campground

T

N

To Heise

Snake River

0   1
MILES

Riding the trail near the radio tower on the way to the Stinking Springs Trail.

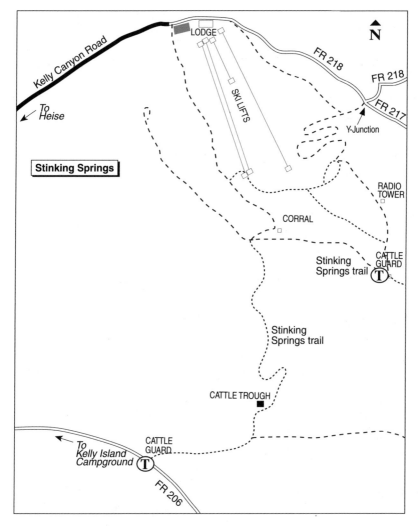

then this trail is for you. Although usually done as a loop ride, some riders prefer the shuttle method and eliminate almost all of the climbing. Use the same driving directions as for the previous trails but instead of driving up to Kelly Canyon Ski Hill, turn right onto the dirt road for the Kelly Island Campground. Drive 2 miles heading upstream and park at the Stinking Spring trailhead on the right.

The trailhead is across the dirt road but instead, peddle back down the dirt and at 2.0 miles turn right onto the pavement and get ready for the long climb! At about 4.28 miles the road turns to gravel and the ski hill is to the right. Continue on to the Y-junction then take a hard right. At about 5.70 miles the cat track for the ski hill is to the right – pass through the gate and follow the cat track as it winds its way up the east boundary of the ski hill. The last portion of the cat track is the crux of the climb so save some juice for this part. At about 6.82 miles the track begins to level off – take a left, ride the two-track for a bit and then stay left as the track splits. A brief climb to the radio tower on the ridge ends the climbing at 7.40 miles; it's all downhill from here! Drop down the gravel road heading east and pass through the gate on the right at the trailhead for Stinking Springs. At about 8.23 miles take a left onto a rocky portion of the trail and hang on as the descent becomes loose and steep for a little while – just keep in mind that the trail really does get better as it descends towards the river. After passing a cattle trough the trail widens and becomes very enjoyable. At 11.5 miles the trail ends at the river road and the parking area.

FALL CREEK CANYON AREA BY SWAN VALLEY

GETTING THERE: From Idaho Falls, take Highway 26 east past the Kelly Canyon turn-off and continue on to Swan Valley. Just before Swan Valley, the highway crosses the Snake River – turn right onto the Snake River Road (FR 076) before crossing the highway bridge, and follow for about 1.5 miles to the intersection with Fall Creek Road (FR 077). Turn right and continue up the canyon. The Echo Canyon parking area is about 1.5 miles up the road on the left. The South Fork parking area is further up the road at about 4 miles.

Echo Canyon to Horse Creek loop

This suggested loop is for the serious hill climber who likes to grind it out in granny gear – to be rewarded with a fun and sweeping downhill on uncrowded singletrack. This ride also works well as an out-and-back ride if you eliminate Horse Creek from the loop.

From the large parking area at Echo Canyon trailhead, ride up through the gate and climb briefly up the gravel road and take a right onto the start of the actual trail. The climbing kicks in as the trail ascends through forested ridgelines and open draws. At about 3.2 miles pass the sign for Deadhorse Ridge and stay right as the trail keeps climbing and tops out on a brief ridge. Pass through the gate as the trial descends and keep following the sign to Deadhorse Ridge. Climbing once again, the trail finally tops out before a steep and loose descent through a poorly positioned gate. After passing through the gate the trail intersects with Horse Creek on the right. Pass through this gate and descend the next 3 miles of fun singletrack that ends at a creek crossing before joining up with the main dirt road. Be aware that this creek crossing can be deep and swift in the early summer. Once on the dirt road turn right and peddle back to the Echo Canyon trailhead at about 7.9 miles.

Rash Canyon to South Fork loop

This Fall River Canyon ride is another classic of the region. With almost all of the climbing in the first half of the ride, it's a great warmup climb with a very fun descent that won't leave you white-knuckled and gripped.

Park at the south fork of Fall Creek right off the main road. Ride up the main road, (FR 077), for 1.5 miles Rash Canyon is on the left with a bridge over the creek; turn left and cross the bridge. Follow the two-track (FR 170), as it climbs Rash Canyon for 4 miles with the last .5 miles being a bit of a lung-burner. At the

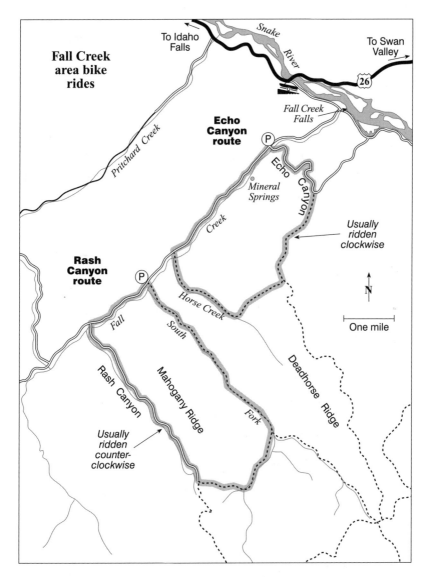

Fall Creek area bike rides

To Idaho Falls

Snake River

To Swan Valley

26

Fall Creek Falls

Echo Canyon route

Pritchard Creek

P

Mineral Springs

Echo Canyon

Creek

Usually ridden clockwise

N

One mile

Rash Canyon route

P

Horse Creek

Fall

South

Mahogany Ridge

Fork

Deadhorse Ridge

Rash Canyon

Usually ridden counter-clockwise

intersection at about 5.5 miles, continue straight over the top and drop onto another two-track that gives way to a singletrack at about 6.75 miles. Another intersection will be found at 8 miles – turn left and follow the trail as it turns into a two-track and descends down through the south fork of Fall Creek. There are at least three creek crossings before the trail empties out onto the main road – the last one being Fall Creek itself. End the ride at your vehicle at about 12 miles.

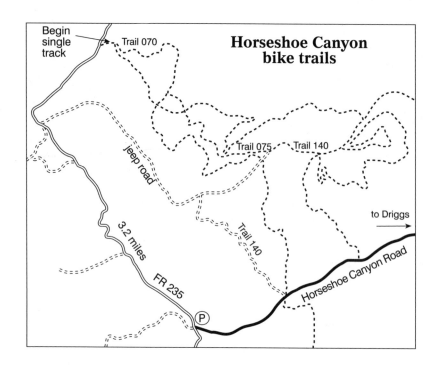

Horseshoe Canyon bike trails

Begin single track — Trail 070

Jeep road

3.2 miles

FR 235

Trail 075 — Trail 140

Trail 140

to Driggs

Horseshoe Canyon Road

P

HORSESHOE CANYON

GETTING THERE: From Driggs, turn west off of Highway 33 at the main street light (this is going opposite of the road leading to Grand Targhee). Follow this road west out of town. After six miles, the road turns north (right) – this is 700 West. When in doubt, stay on the paved road. Go one mile north and turn west (left). After about a half mile, turn left again and follow the road to the end of the pavement and park on the left.

From the parking area, you'll do some uphill grinding on FR 235 for 3.2 miles. After 3 miles, look for an unmarked intersection that drops down into a meadow on your right. On the other side of the clearing is a marked trail (070). From here, the trail climbs for about a half mile. At times you might ask yourself if you're taking the trail in the wrong direction.

At the next intersection, you'll have options. If you go straight, you'll finally enjoy some fun downhill runs before having to do some more climbing.

There are enough trails winding back and forth in this area to keep a biker busy most of the day. After exploring many of these trails (some with ramps for jumping), you can blast down a trail that drops back onto the paved Horseshoe Canyon Road about a mile east of the parking area.

The several intersecting trails can be confusing, even with a map, and may take a few visits to work out the lay of the land in your head.

Riding one of the many trails in the Horseshoe Canyon area with the Tetons in the background.

If you get totally lost, find a trail heading east toward the Tetons and it will eventually drop you back onto the Horseshoe Creek Road.

MILL CREEK

GETTING THERE: From Driggs, drive east on Main Street following the signs to Grand Targhee Resort about 6 miles, turn right onto the Teton Canyon Road (there should be a sign for the Teton Canyon Campground). Drive about a half mile to the winter parking area with a gate and kiosk. From here, ride your bike back to the paved road and go up the hill to the ski resort.

The Mill Creek Trail makes a good loop. Starting from the same gravel winter parking lot near the mouth of Teton Canyon, you can see the sign for Mill Creek Trail. The south end of this trail has been rerouted in recent years to end at the parking lot.

The two general ways to access the trail is to pedal up it (a serious aerobic workout) or to pedal up the paved road to the Grand Targhee Ski Resort and zoom down from the top end. Most people start at the top of the trail accessed from Grand Targhee Resort service road (off the Sacagawea Ski run) and blast down the trail. After about a mile on the service road, take a single track trail that heads south downhill. This trail connects with a two-track road that forks. Take the left hand two-track road that heads steeply down a canyon. After about 3/4 of a mile, the two track becomes a single track and the serious fun begins.

This single track is fast, with only a few occasional flat or slightly uphill sections.

Most of the trail is well cleared and straightforward. There are a few rocky spots to slow down for and a few water bars to bounce over. It is steep enough to get

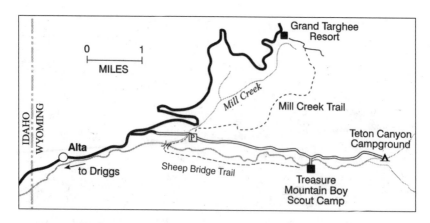

going fast enough to give yourself a scare now and then. This is a good trail to take on warm days because the lower section is mostly forested. In the fall, the trail passes through some colorful aspen groves turning gold.

At the bottom, the trail spits you out on the Teton Canyon Road and next to your car (if you parked at the winter parking lot area).

The entire loop takes about two to three hours.

A couple of caveats, if the trail is wet, wait for things to dry out. This avoids damage that might occur to the wet trail.

The second proviso is to check with Grand Targhee Resort (307-353-2300) before going to see if access is open at the top end of the trail. The resort sometimes does construction work on the ski hill near the trail involving heavy equipment and some blasting. The resort occasionally has other activities, such as road rallies and trail runs that could also preclude a bike ride.

Teton Canyon bike trail (Sheep Bridge Trail)

GETTING THERE: From Driggs, follow the signs on Main Street to Grand Targhee Resort. Drive six miles and turn right onto a dirt road with a sign for Teton Campground. Drive about .3 miles to a dirt parking area on the right side of the road. The trail leaves the parking area on the southeast end.

This short trail begins from the same winter parking area on the Teton Canyon Road about a half-mile from the pavement as the Mill Creek Trail. Some folks call this the Sheep Bridge Trail.

The trail leaves the parking area and heads south on a dirt road. After about 100 yards, the road turns west, but a trail continues south over a nice footbridge, then follows the south side of Teton Creek upstream (east).

This trail is easy going and in good condition. The route is mostly flat or only slightly inclined. A few holes and ruts are evident from grazing cattle.

This trail passes through mostly forested terrain. A few sections go through brush and open land.

After a little more than two miles, the trail turns into the creek and ends. Here there is a shaky, slippery log bridge over the creek. If you cross the creek, you will

Levi Painter blasts through a small stream along the Aspen Trail north of Darby Canyon.

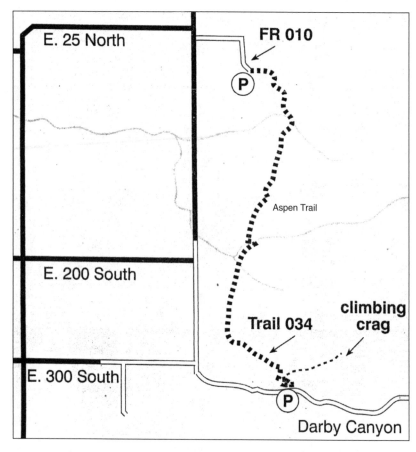

find yourself at the west end of the Treasure Mountain Boy Scout Camp.

The return trip is much faster with the added help of a slight decline.

This is a good trail for beginning bikers, families, tag-along dogs or quick outings. You can also add this short route onto another quick outing to fill out your day.

DARBY CANYON (ASPEN BIKE TRAIL)

GETTING THERE: From Victor, drive 5.5 miles north on Highway 33. Turn right (east) onto a paved road. Look for signs at the beginning of the raod for Darby Girls Camp. After a mile the road becomes gravel. After another .5-mile the road forks. Go right and follow the road for about another .5 mile. Look for the parking area on your left. There is a small, brown plastic Forest Service sign for Trail 034 and a Kiosk. Stick to the main trail heading north for biking. A side trail heading east leads to the climbing crag.

DISTANCE: 4.5 miles one way.

This is a sweet single track mountain biking trail that starts (or ends, depending on your direction) from the canyon and goes north, following the foothills of the west side of the Teton range for about 4.5 miles.

If you're so inclined, you can combine a strength workout with an aerobic workout. Both the trail to the rock climbing cliff and the biking trail start in the same spot.

Bikers call this the Aspen Trail. The Forest Service calls it Trail 034. This trail is all single track and open only to nonmotorized traffic.

At first, some sections of the trail are a bit rocky and may force you off your bike – pushing instead of pedaling. But after about a quarter of a mile of uphill, the trail levels out and becomes a fun and mostly mellow ride. Some of the downhill sections are a blast.

It is important to keep an eye out for other traffic, especially on the fast downhill sections because you can expect to pass other trail users. Some will be coming from the north to south direction. On a given weekend you might encounter trail runners, horseback riders and, of course, other bikers.

Because horses use the trail, having a front fender on your bike is a useful accessory to keep flying manure out of your face.

Most of the trail passes through forested country, which makes the ride a bit cooler on hot, sunny days. Occasionally, the trail opens up to some views of Teton Valley.

Another word of advice: The mosquitoes are often present in late spring and early summer.

Many people ride the trail from north to south because there's a large, accommodating parking area at the trail's north end. If you wish to ride it both ways, riding it from north to south, then south to north back to your vehicle is probably preferable. The south to north direction offers plenty of fun downhill.

SKIING

KELLY CANYON SKI TRAILS

GETTING THERE: From Idaho Falls drive east on Highway 26 for about 16 miles and turn left at the signs for Kelly Canyon Ski Hill and Heise Hot Springs – continue following the signs to the ski hill. At 3 miles, turn right after crossing the Snake River and continue past the hot springs, past the golf course on your right and continue all the way up to Kelly Canyon Ski Hill. About 100 yards before the main entrance to the resort is a parking area on the right for Nordic skiers.

If you're just getting started with cross-country skiing or you're an old hand and want a place nearby, the Kelly Canyon area is hard to beat.

Winter transforms the summertime hiking and mountain biking trails throughout the Kelly Mountain area into some of the best ski trails in the area – and it's all within a half-hour's drive of Idaho Falls. The area is just east of Heise Hot Springs resort off Highway 26 in the Targhee National Forest.

Most of the 20-plus miles of trails start near the "Y Junction" 1.25 miles up the hill from the Kelly Canyon Ski Lodge. Skiing up the hill to the Y Junction can be a bit daunting for beginners, but experienced skiers usually find this section to be a good warm up.

Before you get to the Y Junction, pick up a map at the sign-in post. Don't forget to sign-in. The Forest Service and other groups use these sign-ins to determine the amount of use the area receives. A new map is useful because the Idaho Falls Ski Club is constantly tweaking and updating these trails.

At the junction, you have the immediate option of one of four trails: Tyro Loop, the logging road to the warming hut, Kelly Mountain or the Buckskin-Morgan Loop. A little farther away are three other main routes: Hawley Gulch Overlook, Hawley Gulch Loop and Hawley Gulch Upper Trail. Other adventurous trips can include Stinking Springs on the southside of Kelly Mountain (when there's enough snow), the road to Table Rock Campground and the Wolverine Creek Trail.

Most of the trails in this area are protected from snowmobilers by gates at the ski resort and on the Snake River Road, but occasionally a few sneak through and mess up the trails.

The Kelly Canyon trails aren't a place for solitude, at least not on the weekends. But you should have the trails mostly to yourself after about the second or third mile. This area is well-forested with fir and aspen. Keep a lookout for deer, moose, occasional songbirds and small mammals. Deer are often seen not far from the ski resort. Moose hang out not far from the Y Junction.

Here's a summary of the trails shown on the map:

Tyro Loop

This is a one-mile route that starts just behind the sign at the top of Y Junction. This trail is rated easy, but it is often not groomed.

Kelly Mountain Area

This area follows a jeep trail to the top of Kelly Mountain. The route switchbacks up the mountainside and tops out near the No. 4 chair lift and continues east along the mountain ridge. This area is not marked and rarely patrolled. It is popular with telemark skiers looking for some nice downhill slopes. This trail is rated most difficult.

Buckskin-Morgan Ridge

This 5-mile route heads up from the Y Junction to Morgan Summit. Most people head up the steep section of the trail to the ridge and return via the north loop in clockwise fashion. The northern section of the loop sees some snowmobile activity. This trail is rated more difficult.

Hawley Gulch Loop

This 5-mile route takes you through some nice backcountry that receives less use. Head down the road from the Y Junction toward Table Rock Campground. Less than a mile down the road you will see the Hawley Gulch trailhead on the left. This trail eventually leads into a steep-sided canyon (the gulch) that circles around to Morgan Summit.

Be aware that small avalanches can be present in the gulch. More expert skiers may enjoy taking this trail in the other direction. From this direction the trail is a

A range of trail options await skiers from Kelly Canyon's Y Junction.

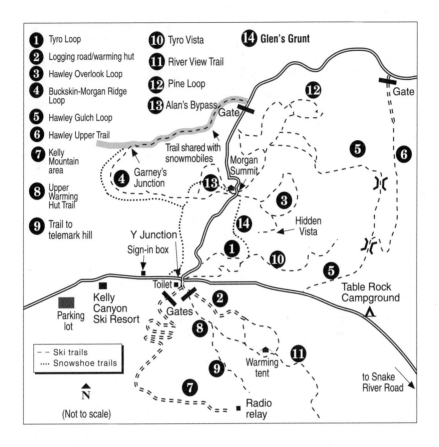

1 Tyro Loop
2 Logging road/warming hut
3 Hawley Overlook Loop
4 Buckskin-Morgan Ridge Loop
5 Hawley Gulch Loop
6 Hawley Upper Trail
7 Kelly Mountain area
8 Upper Warming Hut Trail
9 Trail to telemark hill
10 Tyro Vista
11 River View Trail
12 Pine Loop
13 Alan's Bypass
14 Glen's Grunt

Gate
Trail shared with snowmobiles
Garney's Junction
Morgan Summit
Hidden Vista
Y Junction
Sign-in box
Toilet
Kelly Canyon Ski Resort
Parking lot
Gates
Warming tent
Table Rock Campground
to Snake River Road
Radio relay

- - Ski trails
.... Snowshoe trails

N
(Not to scale)

wild, downhill blast on skinny skis. I would not advise taking this trail on hard, icy snow. This trail is rated most difficult.

Hawley Upper Trail

This route is really a longer, kinder, gentler alternative to the Hawley Gulch Loop that avoids the steep canyon route. The trail is rated more difficult.

Hawley Overlook

This is a short side loop that is mostly level at the top of Morgan Summit. The trail takes you to the rim of Hawley Gulch and offers some very nice views of the surrounding country. This trail is rated easy to moderate.

Hut trails

These relatively easy trails loop to the warming hut set up by the Idaho Falls Ski Club. To the south of the warming hut is a popular slope for tele skiers.

The warming hut at the end of the hut trails is available for overnight stays by reservation.

River View Trail

This trail contours around the west end of Kelly Mountain for some nice views of the Snake River and Antelope Flats beyond. It can also be used to get above the tele ski hill.

For information on snow and trail conditions, contact the Eastern Idaho Visitor Center at 523-1010 or Kelly Canyon Ski Resort at 538-6261 or access the Idaho Falls Ski Club Web site.

HARRIMAN STATE PARK

GETTING THERE: From Ashton, Idaho, drive north on Highway 20 about 20 miles. The turnoff for the park is before you come to State Road 47. The park headquarters is about .5 miles from the highway. A per-vehicle entrance fee is charged and a grooming fee is charged per skier.
DISTANCE: Loop trails range from 2.5 miles to 12 miles.
ELEVATION: About 6,100 feet at the park headquarters; a bit more than 6,500 feet along the Ridge Loop Trail.
DIFFICULTY: Most trails are easy, except for distances. The Ridge Loop trail is rated "most difficult" by the park.
SEASON: Skiing: From late November to early April depending on the snow. Most of the trails are open for summer use by Memorial Day.

Harriman State Park is a class act when it comes to providing quality Nordic skiing and summer-use trails near Island Park, Idaho.
With 21 miles of trails, the skier or biker or horseback rider can make several trips to the park and still have things yet to discover. Harriman's trails take you along the Henry's Fork of the Snake River, around beautiful Silver Lake and through forested ridges and into the Harriman Wildlife Refuge.
The park originally was land owned by several officials of the Oregon Short-line Railroad. The property was the private retreat of such wealthy families as the

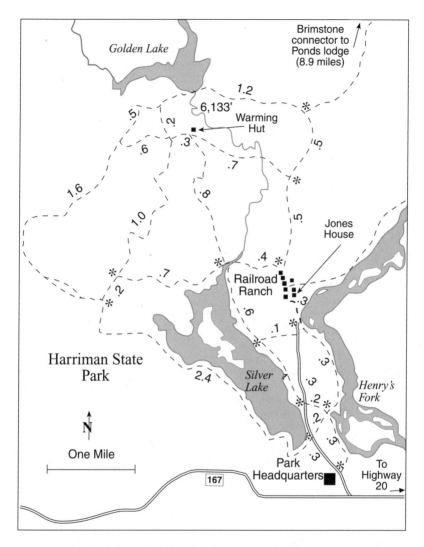

Golden Lake

Brimstone
connector to
Ponds lodge
(8.9 miles)

1.2

6,133'

Warming
Hut

.5
.2
.6
.3
.7

1.6
.8
1.0
.5

Jones
House

.4

Railroad
Ranch

.7
.3

.6
.2

.1

Harriman State
Park

2.4

Silver
Lake

.3
.3
.2
.2
.3
.3

Henry's
Fork

N

One Mile

167

Park
Headquarters

To
Highway
20

Harrimans of Union Pacific Railroad and the Guggenheims, who were prominent copper mine holders. For 75 years, the private land holdings were maintained as a healthy hunting reserve and working cattle ranch. Today, 27 of the original railroad ranch buildings, from the cookhouse to the horse barn, are still intact, furnished, and carefully maintained.

Activities include excellent fishing along the Henry's Fork for cutthroat trout and superior wildlife viewing along the lakes, creeks and river bottom. Harriman is one of the prime wintering sites in North America for endangered trumpeter swans. Also look for Canada geese, ducks, eagles, elk, deer and coyotes. Bring along a pair of binoculars.

The park is day-use only unless you make prior arrangements to rent one of the

75

cabins at the Railroad Ranch. The park also has two yurts for overnight rental. The park begins taking reservations Oct. 1 for the following year.

In the winter, cross-country ski trails begin at the park's headquarters building. On weekends, a warming hut is open at the railroad ranch area. Coffee and hot chocolate are served. Snow in the Harriman area during mid-winter (January) averages around 4 feet deep.

A variety of difficulties are offered among the park's seven loop trails. Most are fairly flat, except for the Ridge Loop trail which gains 400 feet in its 7 miles. The Ridge Loop trail offers the best views and the best chance at solitude on weekends. But the Ridge Loop is not always groomed. All trails are marked.

Of the several possible routes to try out, don't pass up the trail along the Henry's Fork. The Thurmon Creek Loop is also enjoyable. It passes through ups and downs and in and out of patches of forest. The dominant tree at Harriman is lodgepole pine.

During the summer months, the same trails used for skiing are used for hiking, biking and horseback riding. This is a wonderful area to visit during the fall. The park has some patches of aspens, willows and cottonwoods that add splashes of color to the evergreens. Because many of the pines have been killed by a beetle infestation during the 1970s, wildflowers are abundant along the forest floor during the summer months.

BRIMSTONE TRAIL (POND'S LODGE)

GETTING THERE: From Rexburg, drive north on Highway 20. Continue north past Ashton. At Last Chance drive 4 miles north and look for the Island Park Ranger Station on the right. The Brimstone Trail is about .5 miles north of the ranger station; turn left immediately past the bridge over the Buffalo River. There is a plowed out area for parking about a dozen vehicles. More parking is available at the nearby Pond's Lodge. A trailhead sign can be seen near the parking area.

DISTANCES: The entire Brimstone Trail system is 9 miles long. Moose Loop is 3 miles around; The Eagle Trail is a little less than a mile; Thurmon Ridge Loop is 2.5 miles; Tank Trap Trail is about .3 miles; The Box Canyon Trail is about 1 mile; Boggy Springs is .6 miles; and the Antelope Park Loop is 1.6 miles long.

DIFFICULTY: All the trails are well-marked and usually groomed with the exception of the steep downhill off Thurmon Ridge. Most of the trails fall in the easy category with a few up and down sections. Caution: When the snow is icy and hard, downhill sections can become very fast. Distance can be a factor.

SPECIAL CONSIDERATIONS: Island Park Ranger Station (208) 558-7301. For current conditions and grooming schedules, contact the ranger station. Another excellent map – Winter Recreation Trails – produced by Fremont County is also available at most gas stations and at Pond's Lodge. This color map covers all the ski and snowmobile trails from St. Anthony to well north of West Yellowstone. The Brimstone Trail is a Park 'N' Ski area requiring a sticker to be displayed on your vehicle's windshield.

When most people think of cross-country skiing in the Island Park area, Harriman State Park is probably what first comes to mind.

The Brimstone trail offers the same scenic and wildlife opportunities, but often without the crowds that flock to Harriman.

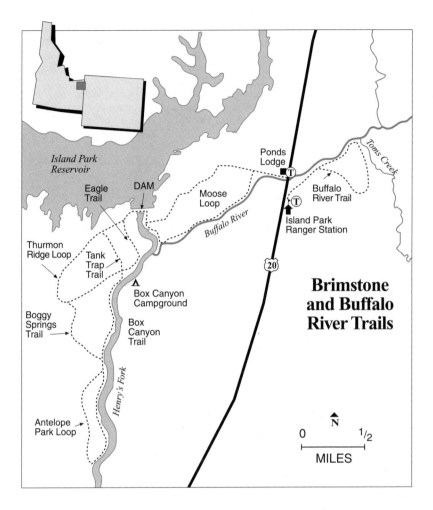

Island Park
Reservoir

Eagle
Trail

DAM

Moose
Loop

Buffalo River

Thurmon
Ridge Loop

Tank
Trap
Trail

Box Canyon
Campground

Boggy
Springs
Trail

Box
Canyon
Trail

Henry's Fork

Antelope
Park Loop

Ponds
Lodge

Buffalo
River Trail

Island Park
Ranger Station

Toms Creek

20

Brimstone
and Buffalo
River Trails

N

0   1/2

MILES

Expect to see several species of waterfowl, including an occasional rare trumpeter swan. Sometimes moose are seen in this area.

The Brimstone trail is a series of loop trails along the Buffalo and Henry's Fork rivers. The trailhead is immediately north of the bridge over the Buffalo River on Highway 20. If you pass Pond's Lodge, you've gone too far.

With all the loops available on the Brimstone trail, it is possible to ski most of the trail with very little overlap.

The first loop on the Brimstone trail is the Moose Loop. This mostly flat trail takes you over to the Island Park Reservoir dam.

At the dam site you will meet up with a few snowmobiles. Most of the snowmobilers come out here to ice fish.

Just beyond the dam crossing, the trail forks. The right side goes to Thurmon Ridge, the left, Eagle Trail.

The Thurmon Ridge route climbs about 200 feet to the top of the ridge before dropping south. At the top of the ridge the groomed trail vanishes. Beyond the groomed trail a sign warns skiers that the 200-foot plunge off the ridge is steep and difficult. This section is often full of deep powder that can swallow up people on skinny tour skis. If you're game for this steep section, you might try mellow, easy traverses down the hill.

You can use the Tank Trap Trail as a shortcut to head south to the river. Just before the next intersection, there is a 100-yard stretch of Tank Trap that is fairly steep. The connecting trail from Tank Trap to Boggy Springs Trail is mostly gentle ups and down until it heads south along Boggy Springs. The Boggy Springs section is mostly flat.

At the intersection of Boggy Springs and Box Canyon keep an eye out for bald eagles flying along the Henry's Fork.

It is possible to continue south from the Antelope Park trail and connect into the Harriman State Park trails. The connection is about 4.5 miles, but the trail is not groomed and often not broken.

The ski up Box Springs Trail is mostly gentle until it nears the junction with Tank Trap trail. Here the trail climbs up the Eagle Trail back to the dam.

After crossing the dam, you can return on the Moose Loop along the Buffalo River back to the trailhead and parking area.

Besides bald eagles, look for a variety of ducks and trumpeter swans. Moose are often sighted near the dam.

BUFFALO RIVER

GETTING THERE: From Ashton, drive north on Highway 20. At Last Chance drive 4 miles north and look for the Island Park Ranger Station on the right. If you cross the bridge over the Buffalo River, you've gone too far. Park at the Ranger Station to ski the Buffalo River Trail.

DISTANCE: The Buffalo River Trail is 2.6 miles long.

SPECIAL CONSIDERATIONS: A Winter Recreation Trails map – produced by Fremont County — is available at most Island Park gas stations and at Pond's Lodge. This is a Park 'N' Ski trail.

If you want to take advantage of the huge amounts of snow often available in the Island Park area, but want some place different than Harriman State Park, Buffalo River is a great option.

The Buffalo River trail offers the same scenic and wildlife opportunities, but often without the crowds that flock to Harriman. The trail is usually groomed weekly and perfect for rookie skiers.

The Island Park Ranger Station often posts a schedule of when trails have been groomed.

The Buffalo River Trail leaves the Island Park Ranger Station and travels north to the river. Parking is provided at the ranger station.

The trail goes upstream along the south side of the river then loops back at Tom's Creek. The trail passes through lodgepole pine forest – the tree that dominates the forests of Island Park.

Expect to see several species of waterfowl, including an occasional trumpeter swan. Sometimes moose are seen in this area.

This trail is basically flat the entire way.

BEAR GULCH-MESA FALLS

GETTING THERE: Drive 13 miles north of St. Anthony on U.S. Highway 20 to Ashton. At Ashton, turn right (east) and drive 5 miles. This is State Highway 47. The road swings left (north). After 4 miles you will pass the Warm River Campground. Continue up Highway 47 another 3.3 miles to the parking area on your left. This is a Park 'N' Ski trail.

DISTANCE: It's 5.8 miles if you do the entire loop trail to the Lower Falls. If you just stick to the rim up and back, it's longer, about 7.5 miles. Add another 3.5 miles if you ski to the Upper Falls.

The main reason for skiing Bear Gulch is the great views. Besides the river canyon below, there's the dramatic view of Mesa Falls.

The trail starts at a pullout off State Highway 47 near the old Bear Gulch ski area. During the summer, Highway 47 is the popular route to view Mesa Falls. During the winter, the road is plowed only as far as the pullout. The parking area is large enough to accommodate several cars and trucks with trailers.

Just to the west of the parking area is the old Bear Gulch ski resort. The hillside still has the remains of a ski lift and a few buildings at the top of the canyon. The ski resort closed down in the '70s.

The ski trail starts at the north end of the parking area. From here the route parallels the road for about 200 yards then shares .4 miles of uphill trail with the

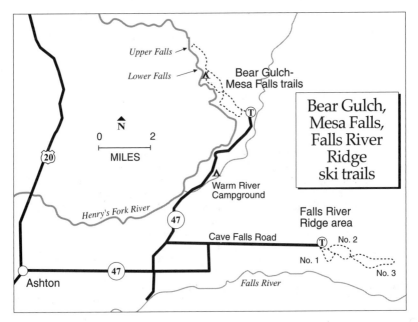

Sam Painter heads out across unbroken snow.

snowmobilers to the top of the Henry's Fork River canyon rim. The first half mile of trail is the steepest and gains 200 feet before settling into mostly gentle terrain.

Once at the top of the canyon rim, the skier and snowmobile routes part. The ski trail is clearly marked by a sign on the left side of the road.

The trail follows along the edge of the canyon rim and presents regular wonderful views of the gorge below. The trail is marked with blue diamonds and Forest Service symbols of skiers or bikers. The route is fairly easy to follow, even when tracks are missing.

Most of the trail passes through thick forest, but there are regular openings that allow views of the canyon on your left (west).

If you continue to follow the rim trail, you will come to Grandview Overlook and a Forest Service campground. The overlook is one of the payoffs for taking this trail. It offers great views of the 65-feet-high Lower Mesa Falls.

Beyond the Grandview Overlook, the trail follows the rim another 1.8 miles to the Upper Mesa Falls. This impressive falls is 114 feet high.

According to the Forest Service's handout on the Bear Gulch-Mesa Falls ski trail, skiers can return via a loop trail that parallels the snowmobile trail next to Highway 47 or return back the route they came in on.

If the skies are clear, don't forget to look east for nice views of the Teton Mountain range if you take the loop trail back.

Keep this trail in mind during the summer months as a short mountain biking route.

FALLS RIVER RIDGE

GETTING THERE: Drive 13 miles north of St. Anthony on U.S. Highway 20 to Ashton. At Ashton, turn right (east) and drive 5 miles. This is State Highway 47. The road swings left (north). After one mile, look for a sign on your right for the Cave Falls Road. Turn right on the Cave Falls Road and drive east five miles to the parking area. Where the road enters the forest boundaries, it is no longer plowed. The trailhead is on the south side of the road. This is a Park 'N' Ski trail.

DISTANCES: The first loop is 2 miles around; the second loop is 3.1 miles around; the third loop is 3 miles around. Loops 2 and 3 are 6.1 miles, and loops 1 and 2 are 3.6 miles for the outer edges.

The Falls River Ridge ski trail is just off the Cave Falls Road 10 miles east of Ashton, just inside the forest boundary.

A large sign announces the trails, and a map is posted next to the parking area. Three loop trails for skiers are groomed about once a week.

Most of these trails are easy to moderately difficult skiing. The uphills shouldn't slow determined beginners too much. The first part of the trail takes you through open terrain, then goes through a mix of aspen and lodgepole pine forest. The trail at times winds through a narrow path cut through thick forest. There are enough trails here to keep you busy for most of a day.

TETON CANYON

GETTING THERE: Take the main street heading east from Driggs (follow the signs to Grand Targhee Ski Resort) and stay on that road for about 5 miles. Look for the Teton Canyon Campground sign and turn right onto the gravel road going up the canyon. The fun starts when you leave the pavement. This road is plowed for about .5 miles to a parking area. It helps to have a front-wheel drive or four-wheel drive vehicle to get to the parking area in case the snowplow hasn't been through recently.

In recent years, the road into Teton Canyon east of Driggs up to the Teton Creek Trailhead has been groomed for skate skiing and classic skiing.

Teton Canyon offers safe and scenic miles of skiing. Another excuse for skiing up Teton Canyon is ice climbing. The canyon walls boast some challenging frozen

81

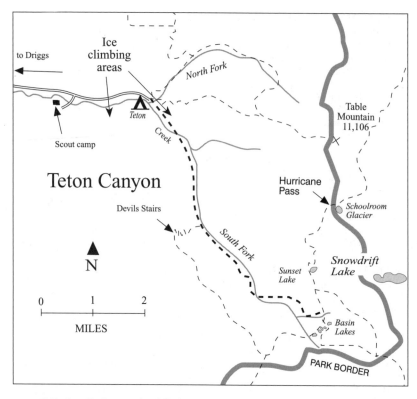

waterfalls for climbers to lead and top rope.

From the winter parking area, the canyon is wide and the views are super. On a clear day you can see the Grand Teton and some of its neighbors above the canyon to the east. On the north side of the canyon, brush and aspens dominate the slopes. On the south side slopes, the canyon is green with a thick fir forest.

Moose are plentiful along the north slopes from the parking area to the trail-head.

The ski trail up Teton Canyon follows the road. If you arrive after a recent snowfall, you may be breaking your own trail. From the parking area to the mouth of the canyon is about 3.5 miles. But the route is fairly flat and quick for skiers.

If you've visited this canyon in the summer months on hiking or camping trips you might not recognize it during the winter. The canyon changes personality. The blanket of white will have you seeing everything anew.

At the mouth of the canyon the road ends and trails enter the Jedediah Smith Wilderness. This is the beginning of the Table (Rock) Mountain Trail and the trail to Alaska Basin. Most people turn back here. The canyon narrows and features several side chutes for the next 10 miles. Many of these chutes avalanche regularly during the winter.

About a mile past the Treasure Mountain Boy Scout Camp on the south side of the canyon is a series of frozen waterfalls popular with ice climbers. There are also a few frozen falls on the north side of the canyon about a third of a mile from the trailhead restroom. Top ropes can be set up on these frozen falls.

MOOSE CREEK

GETTING THERE: From Victor, Idaho, drive 3 miles southeast on Highway 33 and turn left on the Moose Creek Road; drive .3 miles and turn right (east) and drive to the end of the road and park.

DISTANCE: 4.4 miles up to Moose Meadows; 5.8 miles to the falls; 8 miles to Moose Lake.

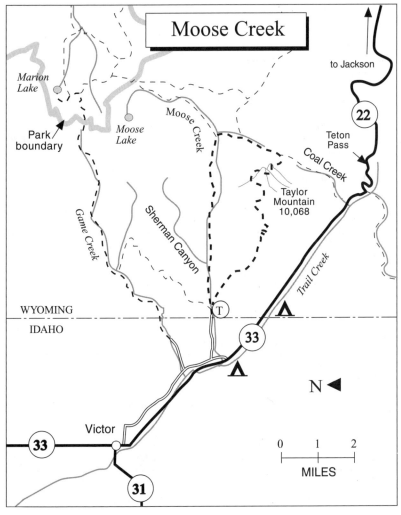

A moose hangs out along Mail Cabin Creek near the ski trail.

Moose Creek is a popular summertime trail and has a loyal following among the Nordic crowd, too.

There are two main users of this trail: The hard-core backcountry skiers who go all the way up to Taylor Mountain (to or from the Coal Creek Trailhead) and the mellower cross-country skiers out for a few miles.

The trailhead is 2.5 miles past Victor off Highway 38. Turn left onto the Moose Creek Road and drive to the end of the plowed section. The road is plowed only to the Moose Creek ranch. During the summer this ranch rents horses for a popular trip up the canyon into the Jedediah Smith Wilderness Area.

Park along the road and begin skiing up the unplowed road. After about a mile the road ends and the trail section begins. The trail forks, with the right-hand trail going up the difficult route to Taylor Mountain (7 miles). Climbing skins for your skis are advisable. This trail eventually connects with the Coal Creek Trail.

Many skiers stay to the left and continue along the creek. The trail forks again after a couple hundred yards. The right trail follows the summer hiking trail and can be steep in places. This route mainly appeals to snowshoers. The left-hand trail crosses the creek on a wide log and winds through a patch of willows to come out on the north side of the canyon. The trail then heads up into a side canyon called Sherman Canyon. Because these trails are all self-groomed, the trail distances can vary depending on who was there last or how far you want to go. The canyon gains most of its elevation gradually but is an uphill workout. It tops out after about 2.5 miles and a gain of 1,600 feet.

The return trip back down this side canyon is a blast.

If you're unfamiliar with the area, a good map to take along is the Jedediah Smith Wilderness Area map (available in plastic).

MAIL CABIN CREEK

GETTING THERE: From Victor, Idaho, drive about 9 miles southeast on

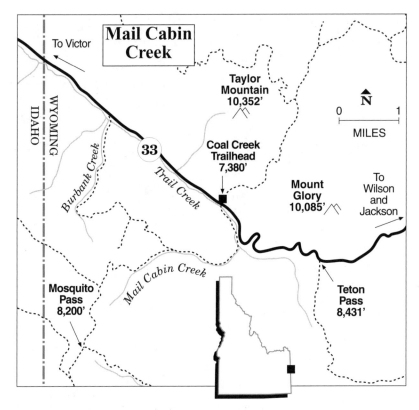

Highway 33. The Coal Creek Trailhead is on the left (north) side of the highway. The trail to Mail Cabin Creek is on the right (south) side of the highway.

DISTANCE: It's about 1.5 miles to the fork in the trail. It's another 3 miles from the fork to Mosquito Pass. From the fork to Burbank Creek is 2 miles. The trail down Burbank Creek to the highway is 1.5 miles.

DIFFICULTY: Mostly easy for the first 1.5 miles. Trail gets tougher beyond the forks. This is not a beginner ski trail, but appeals to telemark skiers looking for good runs.

The ski trail along Mail Cabin Creek starts just across the road from Coal Creek Trailhead, about 2.5 miles west of Teton Pass. There are signs for both Coal Creek and Mail Cabin Creek on the highway. Coal Creek Trailhead is kept plowed out during the winter and is often packed with more than a dozen vehicles on weekends. There is a pit toilet at Coal Creek.

The trail along Mail Cabin Creek is not groomed except by skiers themselves. Because the trail receives a steady supply of users, the trail is usually in great shape and easy to follow. This may not always be the case, especially if you arrive on the trail right after a heavy snowstorm.

For the first mile and a half, the trail follows the creek closely and is mostly easy going. The country is heavily wooded — most of the brush is safely buried under snow.

Ski backpacking near Ski Lake in the Tetons.

After about 1.5 miles, the trail forks. The left (southern) fork continues to follow the small stream of water up a canyon which continues to narrow. After about two-thirds of a mile, the trail becomes too steep for fun tour skiing. Climbing skins are needed beyond this point.

If you continued to follow this trail, it would eventually lead to Mosquito Pass. This pass is technically on the crest of the Snake River Range. This area is where the Teton Range and the Snake River Range come together.

The west fork trail continues to gain elevation but does so smoothly for about a half mile. After a half mile, the trail begins to climb more steeply and even has a few switchbacks. A quarter-mile farther is the destination of many of the telemark skiers. The trail splits again and leads to some open knobs and rises that offer nice downhill runs.

Theoretically, the trail continues on and drops to the top of Burbank Creek and follows that creek down to the highway. Don't count on this trail being broken in and easy to follow, though.

If you wanted a loop route, you could take the trail all the way to Burbank Creek, then ski back along the highway to Coal Creek, but the route along the highway is not very exciting and is clogged with willow brush along the creek. The best time for this route is under a deep blanket of snow. You would probably have to break trail most of the way. One option is to just hitch a ride back to your car.

Keep these trails in mind for summer visits. Mail Cabin Creek starts out as a short jeep road then quickly becomes a footpath. If you climb all the way up to the top of Mosquito Pass, expect some nice views of the surrounding mountain ranges.

SKI LAKE

GETTING THERE: From Victor, take Highway 33 (it becomes Highway 22 when you enter Wyoming) and drive to the top of Teton Pass. From the pass, con-

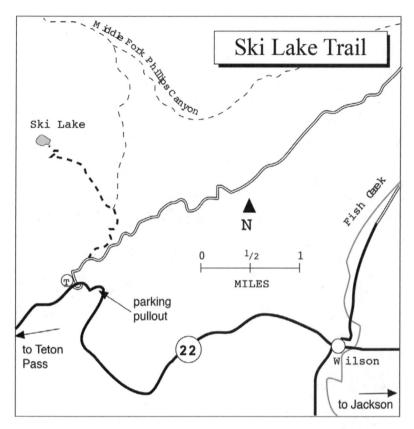

tinue down the highway about two more miles. Look for a sign indicating Phillips Canyon on your left. Park on a plowed parking area about 100 yards down hill on the right. From here, you'll walk across the road and ski back uphill to the Phillips Canyon Road.

DISTANCE: 4.6 miles roundtrip from the highway parking area.

The Ski Lake trail is on the east side of the Tetons a couple of miles down from Teton Pass. The trail starts at the beginning of Phillips Canyon Road. After following the road for about a quarter of a mile, the trail leaves the road and heads up a hill. The trail continues north for the next two miles.

Ski Lake is a good trail to keep in mind for early season and late-season outings because it tends to get its snow earlier than other trails and the snow lingers longer.

When the parking lot at Teton Pass is packed to over flowing, the parking lot for Phillips Canyon Road often has a few open slots. This trail attracts several skiers with dogs – so much so that there is now a doggy poopy bag dispenser next to the Forest Service kiosk sign at the start of the road. If you bring your dog, it's a good idea to bring a leash at least to cross the often busy Teton Pass road from the Phillips Road parking lot.

Sheep Falls on the Henry's Fork in Island Park.

The trail is also used by snowmobilers. They generally stick to the Phillips Canyon Road, but occasionally will ride up to Ski Lake.

The trail is poorly marked and also self-groomed. This can be problematic if you've never been there before and after a recent snowfall. You may start following routes that lead to deadends made by people out for a few hillside runs.

Perhaps the best way to get there your first time is to follow others from the parking lot. Don't underestimate the ski up. The biggest challenge is usually the last quarter mile of uphill before arriving at the lake bowl. With a bit of determination and zig-zag traversing, you can make it. To make things easier, bring along some skins to slap onto your skis for the last steep section.

Ski Lake is not much to look at, especially in the winter. It's a flat area a couple of acres wide at the bottom of a steep bowl. Years of drought has reduced its size considerably.

For those looking for a big day, you can grind your way up to the top of the ridge another 800 or so feet higher and ski back down some monster slopes. Perhaps the more popular way, though, is to hike up from Teton Pass, ski north along the ridge and drop off to the east and come down to Phillips Canyon Road and out to the highway. Here you will need to hitch-hike back up to Teton Pass or have a shuttle car parked at the Phillips Canyon parking area.

SHEEP FALLS

GETTING THERE: Drive 8 miles north of Ashton on Highway 20 and turn right (east) onto a dirt road. Look for a sign on the highway that says "Sheep Falls."

DISTANCE: It's 3 miles from the pavement to the Sheep Falls Trailhead and another .75 miles on the footpath to the falls.

DIFFICULTY: Mostly easy. The trail is tough to bike, though.

In the summertime, Sheep Falls is a great half-day trip or picnic destination, especially if you like to fish or mountain bike. But in winter, the road and trail to the falls makes a nice day-trip on skis or snowshoes.

Most people driving north from Ashton zoom right past the "Sheep Falls Road," sign on Highway 20. If you're one of those who have wondered if it would be worth your time to slow down and take a right turn, then read on.

The Sheep Falls Road, like many of the roads in the Island Park area, can be used year 'round.

During the summer, mountain bikers will want to pull off the highway, park and ride the 2.5 miles to the Sheep Falls Trailhead. The half-mile footpath down to the falls can be negotiated by expert mountain bikers, but I would recommend ditching your bikes at the trailhead and walking down to the river. The trail drops quickly and is narrow. There is often deadfall scattered along the way.

Sheep Falls Road, Forest Road 163, is mostly flat and easily driven by the family sedan in summer. The going gets rougher, though, when you arrive at the sign "Sheep Falls Trail" with an arrow pointing down a rutted jeep trail. With care you can drive the next quarter mile to the trailhead in a low-clearance car. At the trailhead is a small turnaround and parking for about four or five vehicles.

The trail down to the river is mostly easy. It descends through a thick forest of lodgepole.

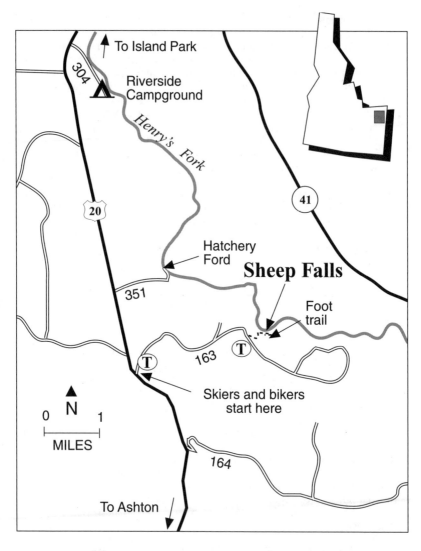

In the winter, the tricky part is finding safe parking off the highway. Often the road entrance is plowed shut. If that is the case, you may need to park at the "historical marker" sign pullout eight tenths of a mile south of the Sheep Falls Road. The next challenge will be following the road to Sheep Falls while it's hidden under three feet of snow. Visiting in the summer first may help.

Once you get to the trailhead for the foot path, you may want to kick off your skis and strap on snowshoes to negotiate the steeper sections. Expect the six-mile round trip to take a few hours.

Because this route is not groomed as a regular ski trail, no Park N' Ski sticker is required for skiers.

Sheep Falls offers two main attractions: Beauty and fishing. The Henry's Fork River makes two big drops – about 10 to 15 feet – around 100 yards apart. The water tumbles over huge lava rocks and continues down a narrow canyon with deep vertical walls. The water is loud and exhilarating. There are some nice perches to stand on to view the two falls and eat lunch.

Between the two drops are some inviting pools and slack water for fishing. Above the first fall are some nice straight runs of water worth trying also. Below the second fall is nothing but impassable vertical walls. If you hike downstream far enough, you will eventually come to some other approachable sections of river. Upstream is more immediately accessible.

This area, like most of Island Park, has abundant wildlife. If you're the first ones down to the river, expect to spook up waterfowl. There is also moose, deer, elk and small mammals.

MINK CREEK

GETTING THERE: From Pocatello, drive south on Interstate 15 for 10 miles and take the exit to Portneuf. Follow the signs to Mink Creek Recreation Area. Drive 5 miles from Portneuf south up the Bannock Highway to Cherry Springs Natural Area. Drive 2 miles south of Cherry Springs and turn left (east) and follow the signs to Scout Mountain Campground and Crestline Trailhead. Drive 4 miles south on Bannock Highway from Cherry Springs to the Valve House Draw and West Mink Creek trailheads. West Mink Creek is on the west side of the road about 50 yards south from the Valve House Draw trailhead which is on the east side. There is no sign that says, West Mink Creek. There is a small Forest Service sign with the number 059. Valve House Draw has a large gate at the trailhead. Its Forest Service number is 5171.

DISTANCES: The Scout Mountain Campground to Crestline Trailhead is 13.5 miles. Add 4 miles if you go to the top of Scout Mountain. West Mink Creek to its junction with Gibson Jack is 6 miles. Valve Spring Draw to its junction with the trail south of Scout Mountain is 7.5 miles.

Just south of Pocatello off Interstate 15 near Portneuf is the Mink Creek Recreation Area. This area features year-round attractions, including: camping, hiking, biking, horseback riding, skiing, snowmobiling and other outdoor activities. If you like the outdoors, this area is worth checking out.

The Mink Creek Recreation Area boasts several trailheads and the Scout Mountain Forest Service campground. There are also two self-guided short nature trails at the Cherry Springs Natural Area and one near the Scout Mountain amphitheater.

The Mink Creek area is a Park 'n' Ski area which requires you to display the Park 'n' Ski sticker on your vehicle when you park at trailheads. You can purchase them at most sporting goods stores.

The area has six snowmobile and ski trailheads. The trails are well marked to keep machines and skiers apart as much as possible. With its close proximity to Pocatello, you can expect to share the trail with other skiers. As expected, the area sees more use on the weekends. If you start out fairly early in the morning you can get a jump on the crowds and reach farther into the backcountry.

A challenging all-day loop trail is from East Mink Creek trailhead up to Scout

Mountain Campground over some ridges and back down Valve House Draw. Expect the going to be easy to moderate until you get past the campground.

If you're looking for some easier routes, try the West Mink Creek trail or the Valve House Draw trail. Both routes have some uphill climbs, but the routes offer some mellower skiing. Keep in mind that these routes can become tougher and scarier when the snow ices up.

Before you go, get a copy of the Caribou Forest Service Pocatello District map to see which trails are shared with snowmobiles. The map also has a helpful rating system for what level of difficulty to expect on the various trails.

OTHER AREA SKI TRAILS NEAR MINK CREEK

Gibson Jack

Drive toward the Mink Creek/Scout Mountain Area on the Bannock Highway. Just across from the entrance to the Pocatello Country Club about 4 miles from town, turn right on Gibson Jack Road. Drive to the end of the plowed road.

This trail stays on the road and follows the north side of Gibson Jack Creek. The skiing is generally easy to moderate until the road ends and becomes a trail. The trail follows the creek and begins to climb and become more moderate skiing. This route eventually climbs to a saddle and drops into the West Fork of Mink Creek.

If you have another vehicle parked at the West Fork of Mink Creek trailhead, you can pull off a relatively short shuttle on the Bannock Highway. Take along a topo map and compass (occasionally people do get confused in this area). A possible extra hour or so side trip when the conditions are good is to switchback up to the summit of Gibson Jack Mountain. This summit offers nice views of the Portneuf Valley and Mountains — and, of course, there's the zoom back down to the trail.

West Fork Mink Creek

This trailhead (a Park and Ski trail) is near the turnoff to the Scout Mountain Road. Look for a large plowed parking area on the right side of the road as you drive up the Bannock Highway. This trail is popular with skiers in the winter and hikers and bikers in the summer. The trail starts on the West Fork Road, but turns into a trail after passing a gate about 100 yards up. After about 2.5 miles of forested area, the trail passes through a meadow with beaver dams and ponds. From here, some skiers head south into the Elk Meadow area or continue to follow the West Fork creek over the divide and into the Gibson Jack drainage. If you plan on making connections with the Gibson Jack Trail, it's a good idea to bring along a map and compass.

This trail can become icy, particularly in the late season. This trail does not allow dogs.

Valve House Draw

Park at the West Fork Mink Creek Trailhead (a Park and Ski trail) and walk across the Bannock Highway to the east side of the road.

92

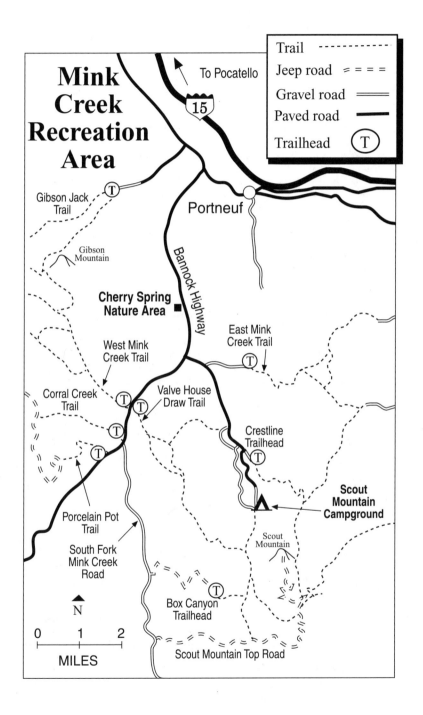

Mink Creek Recreation Area

Trail ----------
Jeep road = = = =
Gravel road ======
Paved road ━━━━
Trailhead (T)

To Pocatello

15

Gibson Jack Trail

Gibson Mountain

Portneuf

Bannock Highway

Cherry Spring Nature Area

East Mink Creek Trail

West Mink Creek Trail

Corral Creek Trail

Valve House Draw Trail

Crestline Trailhead

Scout Mountain Campground

Porcelain Pot Trail

South Fork Mink Creek Road

Scout Mountain

Box Canyon Trailhead

Scout Mountain Top Road

N

0   1   2
MILES

93

This trail follows the Valve House Draw drainage for a couple of miles. The terrain is easy to moderate depending on conditions. If things are icy, expect fast and scary descents.

For those looking for a longer ski, this trail can be connected to the East Fork of Mink Creek Road or with the South Fork of Mink Creek. If you plan to ski some of these extensions, take along a topo map and compass.

East Fork Mink Creek Nordic Ski Area

Pocatello Parks and Recreation maintains a groomed Nordic ski area a couple of miles up the Scout Mountain Road. There are several miles of skate and classic routes groomed. It will cost you to play here — $6 for adults, but the trails are well-maintained and there is a warming shelter and toilets. Occasionally through the winter, races and other events are held here. There are plans to add to this trail system. To get there, drive south on the Bannock Highway from Pocatello and turn left on the Scout Mountain Road. Drive to the end of the plowed portion of the road. Park 'n Ski Passes are also required.

Crystal Summit

For experienced novices or intermediate and above cross-country skiers, the Crystal Mountain area offers a variety of skiing opportunities that will keep you busy for several winter trips.

Crystal Summit is the highest point on the Bannock Highway (the road that connects I-15 to Arbon Valley). Crystal Summit forms the divide between Arbon Valley and Mink Creek. Parking for winter play is in the plowed areas on both sides of the road. These lots are plowed with snowmobile funds but skiers and sledders with a current Park 'N' Ski sticker have also paid their dues and are welcome.

Crystal Summit offers a little of everything: pleasant trail skiing, telemarking and ridge tour workouts with nice views. Snowmobiles also use the area. If you're looking to avoid the motor crowd, the Caribou Forest Service has set aside the Parody Trail just for skiers.

From the parking area, follow the marked ski trail. If you head north you will connect into the Porcelain Pot Trails. Most skiers follow the trail leading farther into the Crystal area. The trail climbs around an open hill called Corral Point. Within 3/4 of a mile from the parking area, the trail descends into a forested area. It then gradually climbs for about a mile and breaks out on a broad ridge with views of Scout Mountain. Telemark skiers can leave the trail at several points to make short downhill trips on the open slopes.

The Crystal trail links up with the top of the Corral Creek ski trail. At this junction you have a few options. You can tele ski on the nearby hillsides, follow the Corral Creek Trail downhill to a shuttle vehicle or hook up with the snowmobile trail which goes to Elk Meadows.

If you don't care about following trails, you can head through the backcountry looking for hillsides to tele ski or just for the views. This may not be such a good idea on days of low visibility. It is easy to get lost when one hill looks like the next. Pay attention to your surroundings whenever you leave the trail.

South Fork Mink Creek

About a mile beyond the parking lot for the West Fork of Mink Creek on the

94

Bannock Highway you'll come to the South Fork Road. This road is a groomed snowmobile trail but both skiers and snowmobilers use the same trail. If you wish to ski this road, a good place to park is in the plowed area at the Corral Creek Trailhead (a Park'N' Ski site).

This is one of those ski routes suitable for beginners. The route sticks to the road and is easy to follow. Probably the best time to go to avoid snowmobile traffic is early in the morning.

Corral Creek

The Corral Creek parking area is up the Bannock Highway about one mile past the West Fork of Mink Creek on the right side of the road (across the road from the South Fork Road). Drive out the Bannock Highway.

The Corral Creek Trail heads west into the woods and is fairly mellow in the first section. The upper end of the trail becomes steep and usually requires some switchbacking to get to the crest. At the top of the crest you can connect into trails that lead to the Crystal Summit-Parody Trail system or just seek out some slopes for telemarking.

Dean Lords rides the Wave of Mutilation, .13b/c, Crank Cave (photo by Nat Meacham).

Climbing

Eastern Idaho is home to many gems when it comes to rock climbing, and what it lacks in sheer volume, it easily makes up for in diversity: If steep pocketed limestone calls to you, enjoy climbing in absolute seclusion at The Fins. If slabby, thin and technical is your game Box Canyon or the Grand Wall will keep you on your toes. Or maybe you're looking for a family-friendly crag like Heise Rock or Ross Park to enjoy a casual day of cragging without hiking. And if you're craving for seriously steep and powerful routes, head out to Crank Cave and climb on the steepest routes you'll find in eastern Idaho.

Climbers should consider these cliffs as local treasures to be cared for and preserved. If we are vigilant in picking up trash, practicing safe climbing and using good manners with landowners, wildlife and each other, the local crags should stay open to all who want to use them.

The climbing season in the area runs from spring to late fall with the exception of the south facing crags composed of basalt – on those sunny windless days these are climbable throughout the winter as well.

The authors would like to point out that the Hot Potato area just east of Idaho Falls has been closed to the public since the last edition of this guidebook and has been omitted.

Note: the authors use a star rating system only to indicate which climbs they and the general consensus enjoy, prefer or downright dislike. Climbers have such a wide array of preference to style that by no means can one person dictate what is a "good" or "bad" climb. You just have to find out for yourself, but the authors feel like the rating system may help.

No star = marginal   * = worth doing   ** = good climb   *** = excellent!

Get the scoop on new routes online at seiclimbing.com

Click on the "Sweet Spots" tab on the left side of the main page to get beta on new routes going in at areas covered in this book.

Eli Watkins on a boulder problem at the Dam Boulders, Teton Dam site near Newdale, ID. (photo by Dean Lords).

Heather Lords delivers some Dark Justice, .12b, at Heise Rock (photo by Dean Lords).

HEISE ROCK

This volcanic plug sits just off the road near the Heise Hot Springs Golf Course. It is also referred to as Elephant Rock or Chuck's Choss Pile.

Aid climbers practiced on this small crag beginning in the early 1970s. With the birth of sport climbing in the '80s, Jeff Hursh started bolting some the most obvious lines on the south side. When Chuck Oddette moved to Idaho Falls in the late '80s, he immediately saw the great potential for numerous lines and quickly went to work developing Heise Rock.

Conflicts with a few local traditional climbers ensued and some of the routes fell victim to hanger theft. When it was all over, the bolts and hangers were replaced and today Heise boasts some of the hardest and best lines in the region.

Spring and fall make for the best climbing at Heise.

PLEASE PACK OUT ALL TRASH!!! This crag sits on private property and the landowners have been kind enough to let climbers use their property for recreation.

NOTE TO CLIMBERS: In 2006 the field on the east side of Heise Rock was leveled to make way for a future RV campground. In leveling out the ground the base of the wall was raised from 2 feet to 5 feet in places making the first bolt on some climbs useless. The original bolt count is still used in this guide but climbers should be aware of this change and use their own judgement when lead climbing – a stick clip is recommended.

One benefit of the leveled and raised ground is that the crag doesn't flood as much when maximum flows of water are released from Palisades Dam during the irrigation season. The area is still prone to mosquitoes in summer. Be kind to the

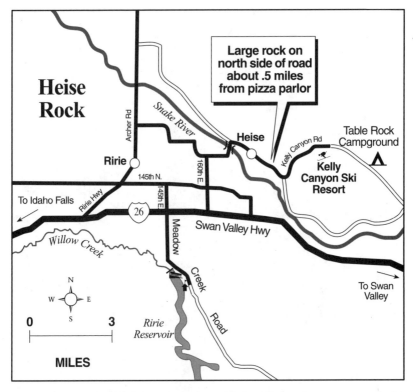

resident bats that live in the crag's cracks and holes. These critters come out in the early evening and help keep the biting bugs at bay.

NOTE TO RAPPELLERS: Climbers have the right of way – the bolts and anchors at Heise were put in by climbers. Check the base of the cliff face before tossing ropes down to rappel. Rappel ropes can easily be moved to the side if they are overlaying a route that is being climbed.

A 50-meter rope is sufficient for all routes at Heise.

GETTING THERE: From Idaho Falls drive east on Highway 26 for about 16 miles and turn left at the signs for Kelly Canyon Ski Hill and Heise Hot Springs – continue following the signs to the ski hill. At 3 miles, turn right after crossing the Snake River and continue past the hot springs. Just past the golf course, Heise Rock comes into view on the left. There is a small pullout parking area directly in front of it – be careful of oncoming traffic. Routes are listed from left to right when facing the wall.

West Wall (afternoon sun)

Two sets of top rope anchors on this side can be accessed by hiking to the top of the rock around the north side trail. The climbs range from 5.5 to 5.8 depending on the route taken. Bring a few slings and some locking carabiners for the anchors.

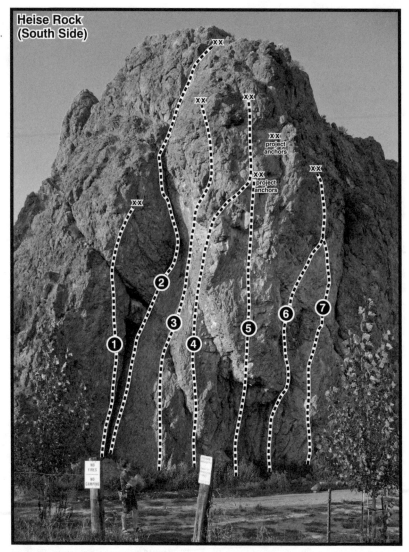

XX

XX XX

XX
project
anchors

XX
project
anchors

XX

XX

② ③ ④ ⑤ ⑥ ⑦

①

NO
FIRES

NO
CAMPING

South Wall (Morning shade, afternoon sun)

   1. Retro Man (5.11a)** – 5 bolts. Face climb to horizontal crack, then over small bulge using pockets to cold shut anchors. Easier if stemmed to the right up to big chockstone.

   2. Pigeon Crack (5.9) – Trad climb big nasty crack. A foul experience.

   3. Hanging Humor (5.10d)** – 6 bolts. Scramble up slippery ramp, traverse right, work around corner up to undercling. Try to hang on through pockets to cold shuts. First sport route put in at Heise.

   4. Little Ninja (5.11+) – Bolts. Squeezed to the right of Hanging Humor.

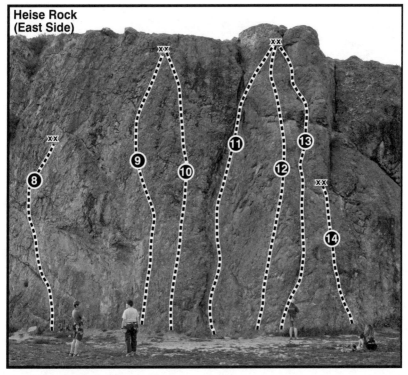

Heise Rock
(East Side)

5. **Rock Ninja (5.13? project)** – Toprope. Start in overhanging crack then up bulge to face to chain anchors.

6. **Seeking Sleazy Squeezes (5.11d/.12a)*** – 7 bolts. Start on jugs, use crack to pull over bulge, face climb to steep pockets then try to hang on through pumpy moves over lip to cold shuts. A classic route.

7. **Wango Tango (5.12a)*** – 6 bolts. Jug start to bouldery section, up to bird crap hold. Continue through somewhat obscure section then left to same finish as Sleazy. A great route that sees little traffic.

East Wall (Morning sun, afternoon shade)

8. **The Devil and Miss Jones (5.10b)*** – 4 bolts. Diagonally left up ramp, then right over bulge continuing to chain anchors.

9. **Born to Rock (5.11c)** – 6 bolts. Wallow through not-so-remarkable moves left of slanted crack to chain anchors.

10. **Butt Rock (5.8)** – 5 Bolts. Fun, juggy climbing. Shares anchors with BTR.

11. **Two Minute Crack (5.6+)** – Trad climb right of leaning crack to chimney, finish on Rock-A-Bye Baby anchors. Can be top-roped.

12. **Rock-A-Bye Baby (5.9+)** – 4 bolts to chain anchors. Possibly the worst bolt line at Heise. Can Be toproped.

13. **Tradmania (5.10a)** – Trad climb thin seam, finish on Rock-A-Bye anchors.

101

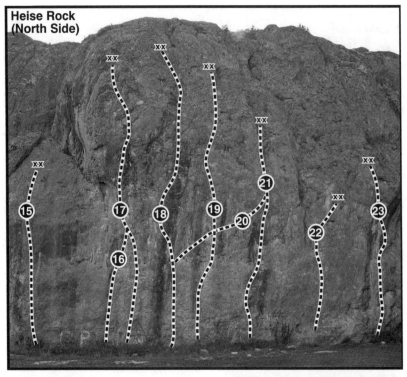

Heise Rock
(North Side)

North Wall (Morning sun, after-

noon shade)

14. Todd's Molehill (5.10b)* – 2 bolts.
Deceptive moves to chain anchors.

15. Clip Me Deadly (5.11c/d) – 3 bolts.
Short face climb over bulge to anchors.

16. Buffy Direct (5.13a)* – Single bolt
start in thin seam left of Buffy. Merges into
Buffy at 3rd bolt.

17. Buffy the Tendon Slayer (5.13a)**
– 6 bolts. Solid .12 moves off the deck, traverse left on jugs to small alcove. Route is
highlighted by main crux at 5th bolt using a
mono to get over bulge to easier but sustained finish at cold shut anchors.

18. Dark Justice (5.12b)*** – 7 bolts.
Power through first crux to jugs. Work
pockets to 2nd crux at 5th bolt. Glide up to
cold shuts. A great route.

19. Wicked Game (5.12d)** – 5 bolts.
Start up flake, power through pockets to big
move to left-leaning rail, to jugs. Finish on

Tom Smartt dances with Buffy, .13a.

102

easy terrain at cold shuts.

20. Traverse From Hell (5.11d) – Start on Dark Justice, through to Wicked Game, to lone gold bolt. Finish on Equilibrium.

21. Equilibrium (5.11c)** – 6 bolts. Powerful moves over bulge, traverse right then up flake/seam. Finish on obscure face.

22. Trad (5.12c)* – 3 bolts. Crimpy moves to enormous jugs. Cold shut anchors.

23. The Bitter End (5.11d/.12a)* – 4 bolts. Move up to underclings, big moves to slopey ledge. Continue up through steep face and finish with awkward moves to cold shuts. A jug at the midway point broke off years ago making it a bit stiffer. Despite its reputation, this route deserves more attention.

PARAMOUNT ROCK

(Morning sun, afternoon shade)

Sitting high above the road, the routes at Paramount offer great exposure and relief from the afternoon summer sun. Chuck Oddette, Steve Reiser and Jed Miller established the routes from 1989 to 1990. While not the hardest climbing around, Paramount is home to great lines in the .9-.10 range – a perfect place for the budding lead climber. All routes except Fly By Night, Positively Negative and Spraypaint can be done with a 50-meter rope.

Dean Lords goes traditional at Paramount.

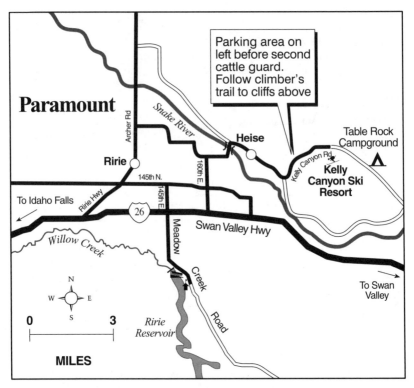

Parking area on left before second cattle guard. Follow climber's trail to cliffs above

Paramount

Archer Rd

Snake River

Heise

Ririe

145th N.

160th E.

145th E.

To Idaho Falls

Ririe Hwy

26

Willow Creek

Meadow

Creek

Road

N
W E
S

0   3

Ririe
Reservoir

MILES

Kelly Canyon Rd

Table Rock
Campground

Kelly
Canyon Ski
Resort

Swan Valley Hwy

To Swan
Valley

GETTING THERE: Use the same directions for Heise Rock but continue on past Heise. Drive past the first cattle guard and follow the road as it turns left sharply and begins to climb – there is a small parking area to the left about 200 yards up the road. Follow the loose trail up to the base of the climbing area. You can also park further up the road to the left in the parking area of Little Kelly Canyon just before the second cattle guard. Routes are listed from left to right when facing the wall.

Parking area below Paramount cliffs off the road to Kelly Canyon.

1. Aerial Boundaries (5.9)* – 5 bolts. Cruise up arete to chain anchors.

2. Aerial-Fantasy (5.9)* – Start on Aerial Boundaries, at second bolt veer right and clip four more bolts. Shares anchors with Aerial Boundaries.

3. Fantasy (5.9+)** –

104

Jerry Painter on Thin Red Line (5.10b).

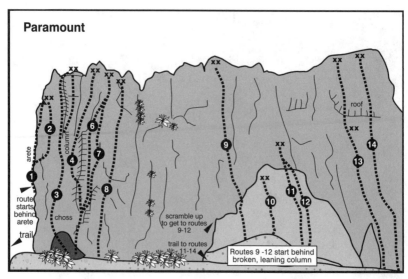

Paramount

roof

xx xx
xx xx xx
xx
xx

arete
column

route starts behind arete

trail

choss

scramble up to get to routes 9-12

trail to routes 11-14

Routes 9-12 start behind broken, leaning column

7 bolts. Start on loose rock, up face, sidepull fractured rock to inside corner left of pillar, then sail through fun moves to chain anchors.

4. Thin Red Line (5.10b)** – 7 bolts. First bolt is way up there but easy to get to. Stay right of the bolt line to second bolt then traverse left out onto face and straight up to chain anchors.

5. Chuck & Jed's Excellent Adventure (5.8+) – Trad climb big inside corner just left of Mr. Rodgers, use last two bolts and chains of Mr. Rodgers. Not shown.

6. Mr. Rodger's Neighborhood (5.9)* – 7 bolts. Climb face just right of Chuck & Jed's to chain anchors.

7. Excitations (5.9+)* – 4 bolts. Clip two bolts at bottom, then place gear in thin crack to the right of Mr. Rodger's, then clip two bolts at top, finish on chain anchors.

8. Wild Thing (5.8) – 3 pitons & 2 bolts. Scamper up face using cracks just right of Excitations. Chain anchors.

9. Fly By Night (5.8)*** – 8 bolts. Climb face just left of broken arch to chain anchors. Best done with a 60-meter rope.

10. Take the Heise Plunge (5.10d) – 4 bolts. Climb overhung section of broken arch. A waste of good bolts.

11. Farr Side (5.10a)** – 6 bolts. Arete climb on positive holds to small ledge with chain anchors.

12. Dark Side (5.10a)* – 6 bolts. Start on ledge just up and right of Farr Side. Climb face to right leaning crack, then angle left to finish same as Farr Side.

13. Spraypaint (5.10d)** – 17 bolts. Climb slabby fractured face to big roof, angle left and over roof using positive holds. Endure face climbing to chain anchors. Midway anchors were added recently making this route more accessible. Route to midway anchors goes at .10b. If not using a 70m rope to the top anchors, 2 rappels will be necessary to lower safely to the ground.

14. Positively Negative (5.11b)** – 16 bolts. First bolt is up there. Climb broken face through small aretes to the double roofs on good holds and sidepulls. Pull over roofs and endure rope drag to chain anchors. Great exposure. 70-meter rope necessary or double 60m rope rappel.

106

RIRIE RESERVOIR

(Morning shade, afternoon sun, no topo)

The climbing at Ririe Reservoir takes place on a short, basalt cliff overlooking the reservoir. A fun place to hang out in the summer, climbers can cool themselves off with a quick dip in the nearby water. The routes are all top-rope only. Long pieces of webbing are recommended for use as anchors. Use the steel poles cemented into the top of the cliff to set up anchors for routes 4 through 6. A 60-meter rope can be set up on two, side-by-side routes.

GETTING THERE: From Idaho Falls, drive east on U.S. Highway 26 for about 14 miles and turn right at the Ririe Reservoir sign onto Meadow Creek Road. Continue for about 3 miles and turn right at the entrance. Go straight past the stop sign, turn right into the parking area. There is a trail to the south of the cliff that descends to the base of the cliff. Routes are listed from left to right when facing the wall.

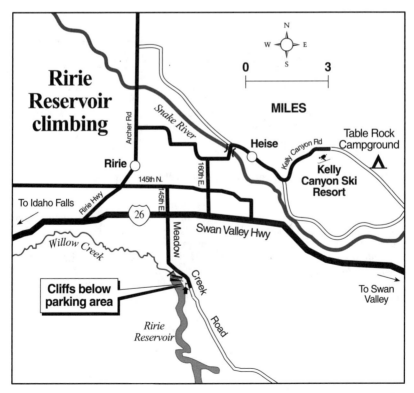

1. **Kings & Queens (5.8)** – Face climbing on left side of wall.
2. **Ririe Gully (5.6)** – Easy climb up gully on the right of Queens.
3. **Battle Of The Bulge (5.8+)** – Small arete climb on the right side of the gully.
4. **On The Roof (5.10a)*** – Climb through main overhang to shelf above.
5. **Aimless Wanderer (5.9+)*** – Climb bulges and cracks to the right of the roof.
6. **White Dome (5.10d)*** – Go up broken face and arete between two roofs using small white dome as a hand hold.
7. **Yellow Jacket Crack (5.9+)*** – Ascend dihedral and then through the right side of smaller roof. Pull up smearing feet and continue on through the crack to the top.
8. **Dean's Torture (5.10b)** – Climb arete on the right side of small overhang and smooth face using pocket on the arete.
9. **Up Against The Wall (5.10a)** – Climb center of face on the left of the small roof then move up sloping face.
10. **Down On The Corner (5.7)** – Climb open book inside the corner.
11. **Howling Coyotes (5.10b)** – Arete climb to the right of open book. Cruxes are moving feet up the smooth face below the arete and first move onto the arete with crimpers.
12. **Smooth Transitions (5.10a)** – Climb face to the right of the arete.
13. **Hanging By A Tendon (5.10a)** – Short overhanging climb with only three moves on the far right of cliff in the brushy area.

BLACKFOOT RIVER CANYON

Local fisherman and river runners are not the only ones who enjoy the long and beautiful Blackfoot River Canyon. Since at least the 1980s climbers have been scaling the tall basalt cliffs that frame the river as it snakes its way westward to the Snake River Plain. Four seperate areas are found along the canyon (in ascending order): The Playground, Desperate Wall, Crank Cave and Rapid Wall

The Playground (Morning sun, late afternoon shade)

In the late '80s, local Blackfoot climbers Jim Neilson and Dean Packum were the first to discover and set toprope anchors on this wall. A few years later, Idaho Falls climbers Chuck Oddette and Dean Lords went to work cleaning and bolting this basalt face and aptly named it The Playground.

Topropes can be set before descending or rappelling down to the base. To hike down, follow the steep trail alongside the irrigation pump or take the steep dirt road west of the parking area down to the river and head back upstream to the base of the cliff.

108

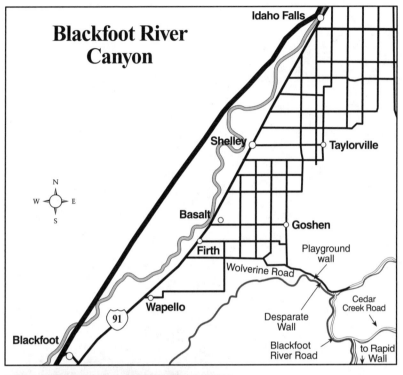

Blackfoot River Canyon

Idaho Falls

Shelley

Taylorville

Basalt

Goshen

Firth

Playground wall

Wolverine Road

Cedar Creek Road

Desparate Wall

Wapello

91

Blackfoot River Road

to Rapid Wall

Blackfoot

N
W · E
S

GETTING THERE: The easiest driving directions to follow are: Get to the small town of Firth. There are a number of ways to do this. Firth sits directly on U.S. Highway 91. From Firth, take Wolverine Road east for about 9 miles. On the left is a small farm house with mobile homes and a cattle guard in the road – turn right immediately after crossing the cattle guard and park in the dirt parking area. Routes are listed from left to right when facing the wall.

Levi Painter warms up on Anchored to the Sky, .9+.

109

The Playground

1. **Tied to the Whipping Post (5.11b)***** – 10 bolts. Start in columns to shallow open book then through blank section to steep finish at chain anchors. A classic.

2. **I'm Too Sexy for My Lycra (5.12b)*** – 8 bolts. Climb column to smooth open book, over the lip to steep finish at chain anchors.

3. **Toprope Route (5.8)*** – Set between Lycra and Gladiator are TR anchors. Variations bump up the grade but the line of least resistance goes at 5.8.

4. **American Gladiator (5.10c)**** – 8 bolts. Climb columns to small roof, up onto face, shift left to the blunt arete to big rest ledge. Poke the pockets on the way to the chain anchors.

5. **Anchored to the Sky (5.9+)***** – 6 bolts. Start in shallow columns to blocky face. Fun moves up fractured plate, then left below roof and finish angling right to chain anchors.

6. **Cure for the Hangover (5.9+)***** – 8 bolts. Similar start to Anchored but traverse right at roof on big flake and finish in juggy dihedral at chains.

7. **Tequila Hangover (5.12d)*** – 8 bolts. Same as Cure but after fourth bolt climb big overhang with glued-on hold, pull the lip and finish on easier moves to chain anchors.

8. **Tequila Sunrise (5.11a)**** 7 bolts. Columns to bulbous section, then up through bulge and finish on hidden jugs to chain anchors.

Eli Watkins eyes the crux on Tied to the Whipping Post, .11b, The Playground (photo by Dean Lords).

9. Toprope Route (5.8) – Climb blocky face to inside corner, fun moves gets you to the top.

10. Toejam (5.9)* – 5 bolts. Start up broken face to fun moves in small corner and left to chain anchors.

Jeremy Curtis on Anchored to the Sky.

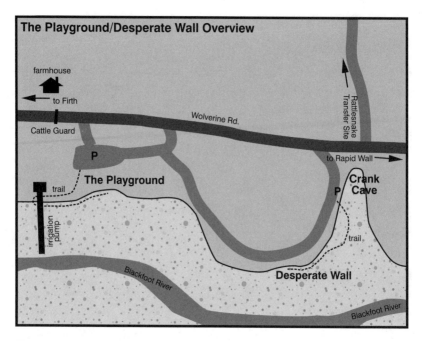

The Playground/Desperate Wall Overview

farmhouse

to Firth

Cattle Guard

Wolverine Rd.

Rattlesnake Transfer Site

P

The Playground

trail

to Rapid Wall →

Crank Cave

P

irrigation pump

Blackfoot River

trail

Desperate Wall

Blackfoot River

Desperate Wall (Morning sun, late afternoon shade)

Another wall developed by Chuck Oddette and Dean Lords back in the early '90s, Desperate Wall hosts some fun and worthy long routes. Not climbed very often, there are still some loose blocks here and there along the routes.

GETTING THERE: Follow the same directions for The Playground but continue past the cattle guard and parking area and drive another .5 mile to the Rattlesnake Transfer site, turn right onto steep dirt road. You can either park here before descending down the steep jeep road or, if you have a high clearance vehicle, continue following the road that skirts the west side of the drainage to the left. Park about 150 yards down the road and look for a gully that cuts down into the drainage. Once in the drainage head toward the river and turn right at the mouth of the drainage. Continue staying by the base of the cliff for about 100 yards until you see the bolts. Routes are listed from left to right when facing the wall.

A view of the cliff at Desperate Wall.

112

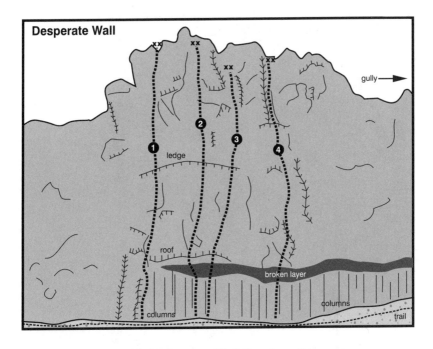

Desperate Wall

1. Cliffhanger (5.11d)* – Toprope. Climb face through to overhang.
2. Desperado (5.11c)*** – 8 bolts. Column/face climb to overhang then up pocketed face. Chain anchors.
3. Widow Maker (5.10c)* – 8 bolts. Named for loose block on route. Face climb to steep finish at chains.
4. The Hidden (5.10a)** – 8 bolts. Climb face to fun steep pockets to chain anchors.

Crank Cave (Morning sun, afternoon sun)

Nestled along the basalt cliffs of the Blackfoot River lies Crank Cave. Originally scouted out and developed by Chuck Odette and Dean Lords in the early '90s, the cave yielded two routes but sat dormant for some time afterward. Interest in steep, cave climbing spurred new development that began in the spring of 2007 by Dean Lords and Matt TeNgaio and still continues.

What makes the cave so fun to climb at is the steepness of the routes and the powerful, yet cryptic movements required to make it to the anchors. It's such a unique style of climbing in an area that is dominated by face/slab climbing.

Being a newly developed area, current route ratings are merely a suggestion and are subject to change. As more people climb at the cave a more accurate consensus can be gathered, but for now the ratings are just a suggestion. Feel free to contact the authors with rating opinions. And please be aware of falling rocks from climbers – do not belay directly beneath someone climbing!

A stick clip is required to winch-start some routes. Please be courteous about the fixed draws that may seem unattended or left behind – these are permanent fixtures on the routes and open for all to use.

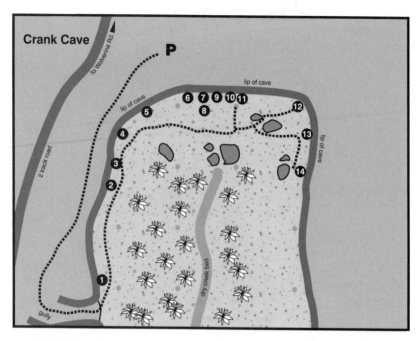

Crank Cave

to Wolverine Rd.

P

lip of cave

lip of cave

2 track road

dry creek bed

gully

GETTING THERE: Follow the directions to The Playground (Blackfoot River), and continue about .5 mile east. At the Rattlesnake Transfer Site turn right onto rough two-track road. Park just off the paved road or drive down the steep dirt road and park near the edge of the cave. Hike south along the west edge of the cave for about 30-40 yards. Descend via a faint trail through a broken gully, the cave is left.

Mike Benson warms up on Powder Finger, .9.

1. Powder Finger (5.9)*** – 4 bolts. Climb nice flake to jugs. Finishes on fun pocketed face/open book section. Sport anchors.

2. Supernaut (5.10a)* – 4 bolts. Bouldery move onto low ledge, then through fractured rock through open book. Ends under small roof. Sport anchors.

3. Drug Train (5.11a)*** – 5 bolts. Either start left of the 1st bolt or winch start to first bolt. Move diagonally right to crux at 4th bolt. Sharp pockets up top. Sport anchors.

4. Bride of Crankenstein (5.12b)*** – 5 bolts. Don't let the choss at the start of this superb route detract you from doing this one, it's a classic! Horizontal moves out to the lip of the roof with a demanding powerful crux pulling the lip. Sport anchors.

114

Matt TeNgaio feeling the Soul Power, .13a (photo by Dean Lords).

5. Free Fallin' (5.11c)*** – 6 bolts. Winch start to first bolt then jug haul through steep section, crux pulling roof. Chain anchors.

6. Excretis Maximus (5.11d)* – 5 bolts. Scramble up chossy mess to gain solid rock. Route veers left then straight up to massive bird shit rest hold. Fire second crux on sharp pockets getting to anchors past the 5th bolt. Sport anchors.

7. El Jefe (5.12a)** – 6 bolts. Same start as Excretis but head right on massive holds after crux. Powerful moves get you to the top. Sport anchors.

8. Love to Burn (5.12c/d)*** – 8 bolts. Start on El Jefe, bust right at 5th bolt and traverse lip of cave for 2 bolts, then finish on Riff Raff.

9. Riff Raff (5.13a/b)*** – 5 bolts. Winch start to starting holds then to steep horizontal hand crack, then powerful moves to pod. Trend right from pod to more powerful moves getting over the lip. 2 bolt hangers mark the anchors.

10. Wave of Mutilation (5.13+ project)

11. Karma Police (5.13c)*** – 5 bolts. This route tackles the steepest part of the cave. Big moves on horizontal roof lead to burly crux pulling lip at the cave. The first ascent was done sans anchors due to anchor and quickdraw theft just days prior to the first ascent! One hanger marks the end of the route.

12. Soul Power (5.13a)*** – 6 bolts. Route moves left to crux at 3rd bolt, to pod at 5th, then power endurance moves to the anchors. Ends in open book under roof. Sport anchors.

13. Crank Addiction (5.12d/.13a)* – 6 bolts. One of the two original routes that opened the cave up in the early '90s. A powerful, techincal start leads to a jug, then more hard climbing. Sport anchors.

14. The Hive (5.11d)** – 4 bolts. Bouldery start to rest under roof. Use crack above roof and bust through some powerful moves on pockets to anchors. Sport anchors. Named after bee hive located to the left of the route in a big hole.

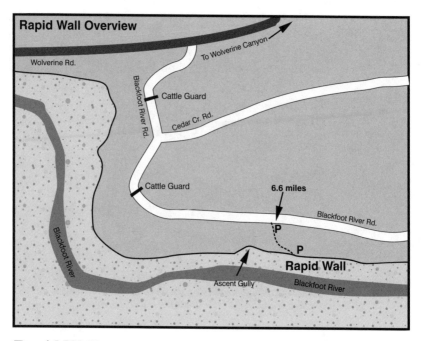

Rapid Wall Overview

Wolverine Rd.

To Wolverine Canyon

Blackfoot River Rd.

Cattle Guard

Cedar Cr. Rd.

Cattle Guard

6.6 miles

Blackfoot River Rd.

P

P

Rapid Wall

Blackfoot River

Ascent Gully

Blackfoot River

Rapid Wall (Morning shade, afternoon sun)

Development on Rapid Wall began in the spring of 2003. Anxious to expand the climbing around the Idaho Falls region, local climbers Matt TeNgaio and Mike Benson found this face that sits high above the scenic Blackfoot River. More development awaits.

Tracie Miller on First Chalk, .10a at Rapid Wall.

GETTING THERE: Follow directions to The Playground and continue driving east. At the intersection of Wolverine Road and Blackfoot River Road, turn right onto the gravel road and set your odometer to 0. Follow the road as it climbs the foothills and heads upstream. At about 6.6 miles park alongside the road and hike out toward the edge of the cliffs. At the top of the cliffs, anchors will be found and one can either rappel from the right-most anchors or brave the steep descent down the gully just downstream from the climbs. This same gully is used to hike out.

This crag is not the best place to bring your dog or little ones because of the nature of the descent/ascent out of the canyon. Being a newly developed area, the ratings are subject to change. Feel free to contact the authors on any upgrade/downgrade suggestions. Routes are listed from left to right when facing the wall.

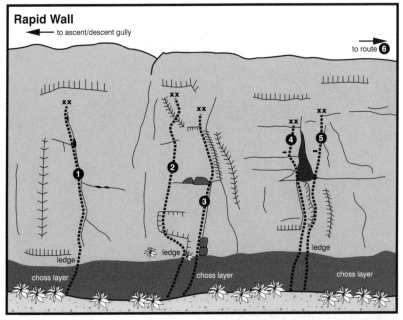

1. First Chalk (5.10a)** – 6 bolts. Start on broken face to ledge, lieback flake to steep face to chain anchors.

2. Ginsu (5.10d)*** – 5 bolts. Up choss, negotiate big flake to face climb to chains at ledge.

3. Lichensmear (5.8+)** – 5 Bolts. Climb inside corner of lichen covered arete to chains at big ledge.

4. Around the Bend (5.10c/d)** – 5 bolts. Climb blocky section to ledge, use flake to get to pockets and face to big jug and crux; end on jugs at chains.

5.Who Let the Bugs Out (5.11d/.12a)* – 6 bolts. Negotiate way to ledge, straight up fin to big rest, fire through crux and finish on .10b section to chains.

6. Under the Hood (5.10d)** – 5 Bolts. (Not shown on topo). Start up face on positive holds, work through crux in right-facing corner, finish on good holds below roof. Chain anchors.

Mike Benson hangs from the sharp edge of Ginsu, 5.10d.

117

Matt TeNgaio on Angel of Death, 5.12a at RPM Wall.

WOLVERINE CANYON

Anyone who has driven through Wolverine Canyon knows that it is filled with limestone – much of it, however, is complete choss and/or vertically challenged. Extensive hiking has yet to produce more abundant quality stone like that found on the RPM Wall. However, there are a few scattered bands of solid rock that hold potential for new routes strewn throughout the canyon. Plus, evidence remains of climbers past: aged pitons have been found in a few cracks, proof that Wolverine Canyon has been known to climbers for decades. Hopefully, with more exploration additional walls may be found that may produce more routes.

RPM Wall (All day shade)

The RPM Wall is mainly blue/gray limestone that is bulletproof and makes for thin and technical face climbing. Yet, the features and angles do vary enough to allow juggy, slightly overhung climbing to exist on a few routes.

Local climbers Mike Benson and Matt TeNgaio started development on this crag in 2005 and continue to further develop the wall.

The crags east facing nature coupled with the dense vegetation at the base make it a wonderful place to beat the summertime heat. The wall sees very little sun and some of the routes stay dry in light precipitation. Fall and spring climbing are both excellent as well. Plan on climbing in complete seclusion as the wall sits above the road and is well hidden from motorists.

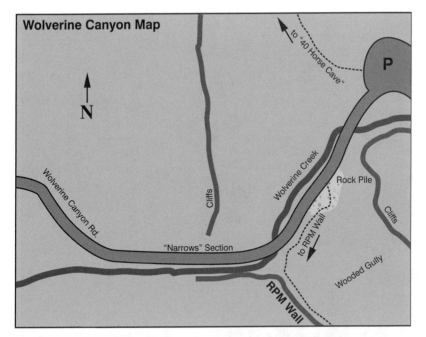

Wolverine Canyon Map

N

to "40 Horse Cave"

P

Wolverine Canyon Rd.

Cliffs

Wolverine Creek

Rock Pile

Cliffs

"Narrows" Section

to RPM Wall

Wooded Gully

RPM Wall

GETTING THERE: Follow the directions to get to The Playground and continue heading east. At the fork with the Blackfoot River Road, head left, staying on the paved road. Continue on until the mouth of the canyon is reached and the road turns to gravel.

Follow the dirt road for about 1.5 to 2 miles. until it passes through a narrow section. You'll know you're at the right spot if you can see the big cave, (40 Horse Cave), up to the left of the road just after passing through the narrows. Continue up the canyon and park on the left side at the big pullout just after 40 Horse Cave.

To get to the walls, walk back down the road about 500 feet to the trailhead. Look for the small pile of broken white rock on the south side of the road – the short trail starts just above it and climbs through the trees.

Being a new area, the trail up to the crag is undeveloped and quite loose in some areas. Routes are listed from **right to left** when facing the wall.

Tom Smartt earns his wings on Angel of Death.

119

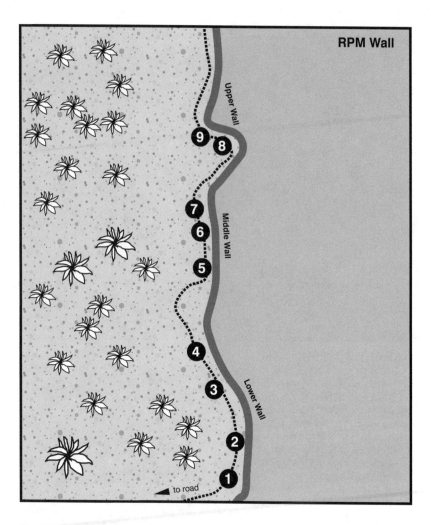

Lower Wall

1. Sweating Bullets (5.11a)* – 10 bolts. Start on jugs then up through crux to big rest ledge. Finish on face with delicate holds. Chain anchors with biners.

2. Angel of Death (5.12a) – 9 bolts. Power through steep start to small rest ledge. Use flaring crack and obscure holds to gain big holds at the anchors. Chain anchors with biners.

3. My Name is Mud (5.10d) – 6 bolts. Hard to read start to slabby crux. Climb right side of the flake to the big ledge at the anchors. Chain anchors with biners.

4. Bombs Away (5.9+)* – 4 bolts. First bolt is high. Start in the small crack/flake to the 3rd bolt. Stay left of the bolt line on the slabby face to the big ledge at the anchors. Chain anchors with biners.

Mike Benson moves through the thin crux on his route Still Life, .12b.

Middle Wall

5. Reach for the Sky (5.11c)** – 7 bolts. Start on jugs then up through crux to big rest ledge. Finish on face with delicate holds. Chain anchors with biners.

6. Still Life (5.12b)*** – 8 bolts. This routes starts just left of the tree. Super thin moves all the way to the 4th bolt. Big jug out right makes a good rest, then fun .10+ moves all the way to the anchors. Chain anchors with biners.

7. Lateralis (5.11c)* – 5 bolts. Hard to read start to fun middle section on positive holds. Main crux at top getting to anchors. Chain anchors with biners.

Upper Wall

8. Freakie Stylie Direct (5.12d)** – 3 bolts. Stick clip first bolt that is way up there. Burly thin moves to slopey pocket below flake, then straight up on more crimpy moves to anchors. Sport anchors.

9. Freakie Stylie (5.12b)*** – 4 bolts. Use seam and traverse right to gain flake at 3rd bolt, then merge with Freakie Stylie Direct. A short but fun route.

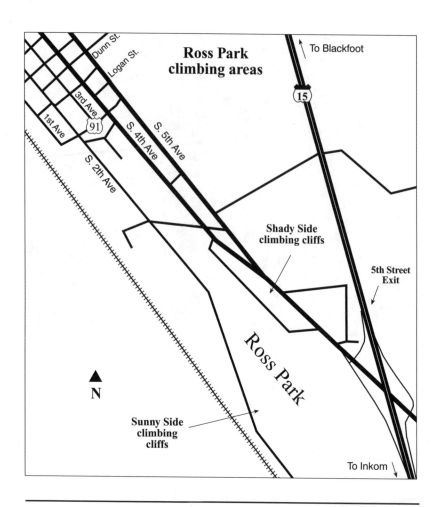

Ross Park
climbing areas

To Blackfoot

Dunn St.

Logan St.

3rd Ave

1st Ave

91

S. 4th Ave

S. 5th Ave

S. 2th Ave

Shady Side
climbing cliffs

5th Street
Exit

N

Sunny Side
climbing
cliffs

Ross Park

To Inkom

Ross Park

Conveniently located in the town of Pocatello, Ross Park is home to more than 140 climbs.

Located on the northeast side of the park, the Shady Side offers toprope climbs ranging from 5.7 to 5.12b – plus many fun boulder problems.

On the southwest side of the park, the Sunny Side offers great toprope, lead climbs and boulder problems as well.

The routes were put in by the Idaho State University Outdoor Club and the area is maintained by the Pocatello Parks and Recreation.

Routes can be easily identified by their numbers painted at the base of the cliffs and/or stamped plates at the anchors on top. There are also a few stamped plates attached to rocks along the base of the cliffs. Once a week during the summer, the outdoor club sets up top ropes for climbers to use in the evenings (usually on Thursdays). Find the ISU Outdoor Club on the Internet for precise schedules of

Sam Painter leads route 63 at the Ivy League Wall, Sunny Side, Ross Park.

climbing nights and which side of the park will be set up. Most routes are short enough that one rope will service two routes.

GETTING THERE: Take I-15 to Pocatello and take the 5th Street exit. Drive west for about 1 mile and the Shady Side cliffs will come into view on the left. There is limited parking along 4th Street. Extra parking is available in Upper Ross Park by the covered shelter. For the Sunny Side, follow the signs along 5th Street to Ross Park, drive through the park, passing the big swimming pool (on your right) and just after exiting on the south side, there is a big parking area on the left.

Shady Side
(morning sun, afternoon shade)
Routes are listed from left to right when facing the wall.

1. (5.9+)	31. (5.7)
2. (5.10a)	32. (5.10b)
3. (5.8)	33. (5.8)
4. (5.8)	34. (5.9+)
5. (5.10c)	35. (5.8)
6. (5.10c)	36. (5.10c)
7. (5.9+)	37. (5.10b)
8. (5.11a)	38. (5.8)
9. (5.10a)	39. (5.10b)
10. (5.10a)	40. (5.11b)
11. (5.9-)	41. (5.10a)
12. (5.10a)	42. (5.12c)
13. (5.9+)	43. (5.8)
14. (5.9+)	44. (5.9+)
15. (5.9+)	45. (5.12b)
16. (5.11b)	46. (5.10b)
17. (5.9+)	47. (5.10c)
18. (5.9+)	48. (5.8)
19. (5.10c)	49. (5.7)
20. (5.10c)	50. (5.10c)
21. (5.10b)	51. (5.9)
22. (5.9+)	52. (5.9)
23. (5.10a)	53. (5.10b)
24. (5.11b)	54. (5.12b)
25. (5.11a)	55. (5.9)
26. (5.11a)	56. (5.8)
27. (5.10b)	57. (5.8)
28. (5.9)	58. (5.9+)
29. (5.7)	59. (5.7)
30. (5.7)	60. (5.11c/d)

Sarah Painter on a .9 on the Shady Side at Ross Park.

125

Sunny Side
(Morning shade, afternoon sun)
Routes are listed from left to right when facing the wall
(routes 1 to 8 are on private land).

Main Wall

9. bolted (5.10d)	27. bolted (5.9-)
10. bolted (5.11b)	28. bolted (5.8)
11. bolted (5.12a)	28A. (5.7)
11A. bolted (5.12b)	29. bolted (5.11a)
12. bolted (5.11b)	29A. bolted (5.12a)
12A. (5.?)	30. (5.10a)
13. bolted (5.10d)	31. (5.9-)
13A. bolted (5.12c)	32. bolted (5.10a)
14. (5.10c)	33. bolted (5.10b)
15. (5.8)	34. (5.10b)
16. bolted (5.11a)	35. bolted (5.9+)
17. (5.9+)	36. (5.10a)
17A. bolted (5.10b)	37. bolted (5.11c)
18. (5.7)	38. (5.9)
19. (5.9+)	39. (5.9)
20. bolted (5.10a)	40. bolted (5.8)
21. bolted (5.10d)	41. (5.8)
22. (5.8)	42. (5.9)
23. (5.9)	43. bolted (5.10c)
24. (5.7)	44. bolted (5.12a)
24A. bolted (5.11b)	45. (5.10c)
25. (5.7)	46. (5.9)
26. (5.8)	46A. (5.10d)

Sunny Side parking lot at Ross Park.

126

Mike Benson looking for love on Ross Park's Sunny Side Wall.

Middle Wall

46B. (5.9)
47. (5.7)
48. (5.8)
48A. bolted (5.10a)
48B. bolted (5.10a)
49. (5.9)
50. (5.11?)
51. bolted (5.10c)
52. bolted (5.10b)
53. bolted (5.11c)
54. (5.10a)

54A. bolted (5.12a/b)
55. bolted (5.11a)
55A. bolted (5.12b)
56. (5.9+)
57. (5.11a)
58. bolted (5.11)
58A. (5.12b)
59. bolted (5.10a)
60. (5.10)
61. bolted (5.10a)
62. (5.?)

Ivy League Wall

62A. bolted (5.10)
63. (5.6)
64. bolted (5.10c)
65A. bolted (5.12a)
65. bolted (5.10a/b)
66. (5.10a)
67. bolted (5.10a)
68. (5.8)

68A. bolted (5.8)
69. bolted (5.9+)
70. (5.9+)
71. bolted (5.10d)
72. bolted (5.9+)
73. bolted (5.11c)
74. bolted (5.10b/c)
75. bolted (5.12a)

THE FINS

Located in the extreme southern tip of the Lost River Range just southwest of Howe lie the Fins. Highlighted by vertical-to-slightly-overhung pocketed limestone that rivals Sinks Canyon in Lander, Wyo., the Fins is truly a unique climbing area to eastern Idaho.

Chuck Denure discovered the area's climbing potential back in the early-mid '90s and bolted a number of lines on the Head Wall and the Warm Up Wall. Hailey residents Marc Hanselman and Alex McMeekin stumbled upon the developed routes and the untapped potential in 1998. They soon went to work bolting several lines on the Discovery Wall and eventually filling in the gaps on the Head Wall. As more climbers visited, the massive potential for new routes was quickly realized. Erik Leidecker, Jeremy Scherer, Peter Heekin, Matt TeNgaio and Dave Bingham have contributed to the wave of new routes in the past few years.

The main concentration of climbing sits at the head of Eightmile Canyon and extends southward following the descending ridgeline. Sitting at about 7,600 feet this is a great summer area. However, the morning sun on the east facing walls can be brutal up there as there is no shade until about 1 p.m. The rock is sharp in nature but offers great texture. The climbing is steep, somewhat powerful and sustained! A majority of the routes are in the 5.12 range, with a few 5.13s and the possibility for 5.14. A 60m rope is recommended but not needed for all routes.

Please respect routes with red tags on the first bolt. These routes are considered "projects" and are either not completely bolted/cleaned or have not seen a first ascent by the route equipper. Project routes that are "open" to others are noted in their descriptions in the following pages.

The authors wish to stress to climbers visiting The Fins: please keep the place as pristine as you found it so others may enjoy it as well.

The entrance to Eightmile Canyon off of Highway 33.

Dean Lords on "51" at the Yellow Cake Wall.

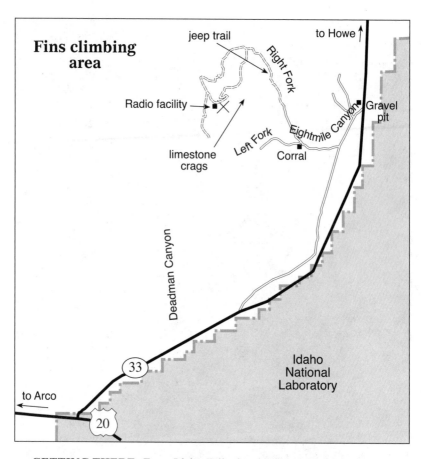

Fins climbing area

jeep trail

to Howe ↑

Right Fork

Radio facility —

Gravel pit

Eightmile Canyon

Left Fork

limestone crags

Corral

Deadman Canyon

33

Idaho National Laboratory

to Arco ←

20

GETTING THERE: From Idaho Falls, head west on Highway 20 towards Arco for about 57 miles. Before reaching Arco, turn right on Highway 33 and drive north towards Howe. At about 9 miles turn left, west, at a gravel pit onto an unmarked dirt road entering Eightmile Canyon. At about .5 mile down the dirt road, turn right through a gate and at another .5 mile veer right as the road descends down a small hillside. At about 3.6 miles the lower parking area is found on the left side of the road and for now only accomodates about four cars. Two-wheel drive vehicles will want to park here. Four-wheel drive cars may continue up the steep road for another 1.5 miles to the saddle, however, this road can be very loose and it is quite steep in some sections. From there, turn left up a two-track road that climbs to a grove of pine trees and an awesome camping spot. Park near the trees and follow the short trail to the Head Wall.

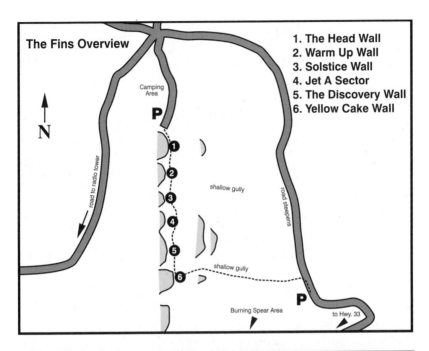

The Fins Overview

1. The Head Wall
2. Warm Up Wall
3. Solstice Wall
4. Jet A Sector
5. The Discovery Wall
6. Yellow Cake Wall

N

road to radio tower

Camping Area

P

① ❶

② ❷

③ ❸

④ ❹

⑤ ❺

⑥ ❻

shallow gully

road steepens

shallow gully

P

Burning Spear Area

to Hwy. 33

Lower parking area located at 3.6 miles from the highway. Discovery Wall is just right of center in picture.

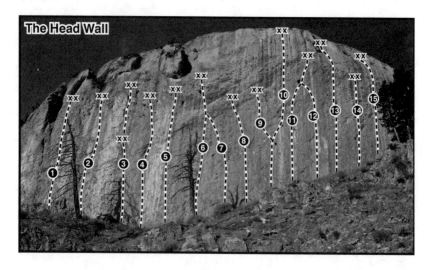

The Head Wall (All walls see morning sun, afternoon shade)

5.12 is the name of the game at this wall. First wall to be developed at the Fins. 2 minute approach from above or 45 minute approach from lower parking area. Routes are listed from left to right when facing wall.

Dave Wirth gettin' high on Clips From the Bong, .12c.

1. Unkown (5.11c/d)*** – 6 bolts. Left-most route on the wall. Start on chossy section to great pockets on white limestone to 1st set of anchors. To the 2nd set of anchors rating unkown.

2. Ghost in the Shell (5.12a)*** – 6 bolts. More pocket pulling on good stone. Chain anchors.

3. Unkown (5.12a)* – 9-10 bolts. Starts by fallen tree. To the 1st set of anchors is .10d, 2nd set about .12a.

4. Seven Arrows (5.11d)* – 6 bolts. Sport anchors.

5. Al's Diner (5.13a)*** – 8 bolts. Main crux down low. Great route. Sport anchors.

6. Bean Fiddler (5.12c)*** – 7 bolts. Start near tree stump. Goes through shallow pod at top of route to ring anchors.

7. Time Will Tell (5.12a/b)** – 7 bolts. Veers left at 6-7th bolt and joins Bean Fiddler.

Mike Benson connecting the dots on Koona, .11d/.12a.

8. Koona (5.11d/.12a)** – 5 bolts. Route veers left at the top to Sport anchors.

9. Middle Man (5.12b)* – 7 bolts. Start on Bong then veer left after 4th bolt. Sport anchors.

10. Clips From the Bong (5.12c)*** – 13 bolts. Longest route on the wall. Pull on pockets for 10 bolts then negotiate slab ending on small holds. Chain anchors.

11. Yukon Gold (5.12b)* – 7 bolts. Straight up then right to big pod. Sport anchors.

12. White Rhino (5.12a/b)** – 6 bolts. Follow white streak then veer left to big pod and merge with Yukon. Sport anchors.

13. Unkown (5.11c)* – 10 bolts. Fun route execpt for last 2 bolts. Bail biners are commonly found on 8th bolt. Chain anchors.

14. Warm up 2 (5.11a)** – 8 bolts. The easier of the first two. Sport anchors.

15. Warm up 1 (5.11b)** – 7 bolts. Right-most route on the wall. Slab ending at chain anchors.

Warm Up Wall

5 minute approach from above or 35 minutes from below. Less than vertical rock. Easiest routes at the Fins. Routes are listed from left to right when facing wall.

1. Unkown (5.7)** – 11 bolts. Long slabby route. Chain anchors.

Steve Bohrer flies up Cicada, .10a on the Warm Up Wall.

2. Unkown (5.9)* – 8 bolts. Start on #1 then veer right after 3rd bolt. Shares bolts and anchors with Cicada.

3. Cicada (5.10a)** – 7 bolts. Direct start to #2. Vertical climbing leads to easy slab finish on big holds. Chain anchors.

To Warm Up Wall ▶

Solstice Wall

Nice tall formation to the left of the Warm Up Wall. 10 minute approach from above or 30 minute approach from below. Routes are listed from left to right when facing wall.

1. Project
2. Solstice (5.12b)* – 8 bolts. Located on the far right side of the wall. Stick clip the 1st bolt and work the bouldery start. Fun climbing on a variety of holds before the crux at the 7th bolt. Watch out for tree at the base of the climb when lowering. Sport anchors.

136

The Discovery Wall - Jet A Sector

15 minute approach from above or 20 minute approach from below. Routes are listed from left to right when facing wall.

1. G.I. Joe Bouncy Tank (5.12a)** – 6 bolts. Follow flake to pockets. Crux is at the top of the route. Sport anchors.

2. Jet A (5.12a/b)** – 7 bolts. Follow seam straight up to sport anchors.

3. Speed Boat (Project)

To Solstice Wall ▷

xx

④

⑤

4. Throttle Gift (Project)

5. Water from Stone (5.11b)* – 7 bolts. Located about 100 yards right of route 4. Follows seam. Chain anchors.

6. Room with a View (Project) – Right of route 5. Has small cave up top.

Heather Lords dropping science on EBR-1, .11a.

To Jet A Sector ▶

The Discovery Wall - The Mothership Sector

A big chunk of rock. Home to the classic hard route Bushido. Routes are listed from left to right when facing wall.

1. Skeletor (5.12c)** – 4 bolts. Get your crimp game on for this one. Sport anchors.

2. Bushido (5.13b)*** – 10 bolts. Classic hard route. Hard climbing off the ground, 2 distinct cruxes followed by power endurance moves to the anchors. A must do for the 5.13 climber. Sport anchors.

139

The almighty Discovery Wall.

3. Bare Knuckle Boxer (5.13+ project) – 4 bolt extension of Bushido that continues past the pod, .12d/.13a on it's own.

4. The Mothership (5.12c)** – 8 bolts. Route angles right then up. Crux is highlighted by a mandatory pinky mono move. Shares anchors with Bushido.

5. Mission Control (5.13 project) – 4 bolt extension of Mothership. Same ending as route 3, different start.

The Discovery Wall - Martini Sector

Named for the martini shaped flake at the top of route #6. Routes are listed from left to right when facing wall. **Note:** Located just down and left of the Discovery Wall on a short, steep and black streaked wall is a 6 bolt route named Sea Monkey, .12a.

1. Chapstick (5.12a)*** – 10 bolts. Great route with pockets, crimps, and slab. Chain anchors.

2. Pure Rock Fury (5.13 Project) – 11 bolts. Sustained crux through lower half of route.

3. The Dinner Roll (5.12c)*** – 10 bolts. Bouldery start leads to big moves on good pockets. Traverses right to Shaken anchors.

4. Shaken Not Stirred (5.12a)*** – 8 bolts. Fun technical crux low on route leads to pumpy finish. Chain anchors.

5. Yellowman (5.11a)*** – 6 bolts. Starts on chossy flake/ledge. Great route on excellent pockets. A bit sporty but worth every minute. Shares anchors with Shaken.

6. Martini (5.12a)*** – 8 bolts. Another excellent 5.12 that ends at the "Martini" flake. Sport anchors.

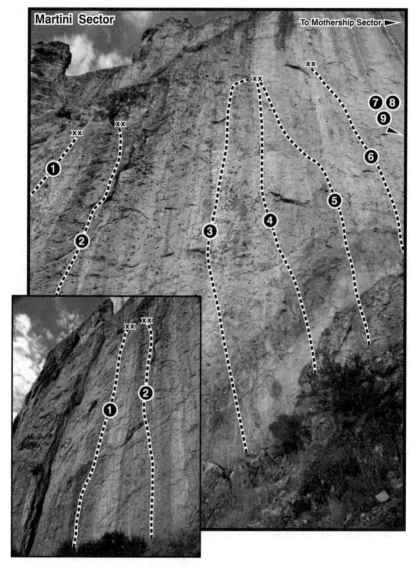

7. EBR-1 (5.11a)** – 6 bolts. Tricky start to big pockets, crux finish. Sport anchors.

8. Route of Discovery (5.13+ open project) – 9 bolts. Route has been red-pointed to the 7th bolt, (.13-), before the big blank traverse to the anchors. It's suggested that anchors may be added at the 7th bolt.

9. Beginners Mind (project)

141

Trail to Lower
Parking Area ◁

Yellow Cake Wall

Yellowish colored wall just left of the Discovery Wall. These routes were put in by Dave Bingham in 2007. 15 minute approach from lower parking area. Routes are listed from left to right when facing wall.

1. Avitar (5.12a)** – 7 bolts. Climb right leaning seam to chain anchors.
2. "51" (5.11d)** – 5 bolts. Climb right leaning seam to chain anchors.
3. Yellow Cake (5.10d)** – 6 bolts. Starts between two bushes and climbs pockets and edges. Chain anchors.

Burning Spear Area

Burning Spear Routes

X-Crack Route

Approach

Burning Spear Area

Located about .5 mile south of the Discovery and Yellow Cake Walls is an area of highly concentrated slabby formations. New route pioneer and Hailey hardman Dave Bingham bolted a handful of great routes here during the 2006 season. Some routes are topropes now but may be bolted in the near future. More development awaits.

GETTING THERE: Follow the main Fins driving directions but at about 3.4 miles from the highway park to the left of the road near a power line with a "Danger" sign. Hike diagonally up and left to a shallow dry gully to a cluster of burned pine trees. The routes are on the tall formation directly above the burned trees.

Burning Spear Wall (Morning sun, afternoon shade)

Climbs are located in a secluded setting. Routes are listed from left to right when facing wall.

1. Burning Spear (5.10a)* – 6 bolts. 1st bolt is tan colored. Chain anchors.
2. (5.10a)* – Toprope.
3. (5.10) – Toprope.
4. Unkown (5.10)
5. Cajun Hot Stick (5.10c/d)* – 8 bolts. Starts just right of water groove/crack. Angles right near the top. Chain anchors.
6. Central Line (5.12 Project)

Burning Spear Area

7. Let it Burn (5.11a)** – 10 bolts. Angles right at mid-way point. Chain anchors.

8. Matchhead (5.11b)** – 6 bolts. Shorter route just downhill from Matchhead. Chain anchors.

9. X-Crack (5.10+/.11-) – 6 bolts. Route is located straight up from the parking area past a small sign on the right side of the dry shallow gully. Chain anchors.

Tom Smartt says "Yes" to Dr. No, .12c/d, Box Canyon.

BOX CANYON

Just north of the small town Howe lies Saddle Mountain. Its southern slopes are cut by fantastic canyons composed mainly of limestone. A fantastic area to hike and explore, the canyons also offer superb climbing possibilities. Alex McMeekin and friends from the Hailey area developed the sport routes out here in the early-mid '90s. With climbs from 20 feet to 500 feet, Box Canyon has something for everyone.

Most climbers new to Box Canyon are quick to comment on the sharp nature of the rock. While the texture of the limestone may shorten the lifespan of one's resole job, it makes for great climbing on very positive rock.

This canyon, as well as several nearby canyons boast great potential for future

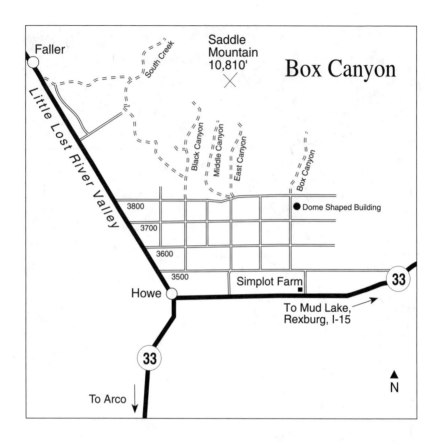

climbing routes. But until the Wilderness Study Area designation changes and the Bureau of Land Management can be assured that archaeological features will not be damaged, new climbing routes will have to wait. The authors wish to stress this strongly. Legally, the BLM has every right to remove all existing bolts and anchors. But, if climbers can demonstrate their willingness to cooperate and keep this prime area clean, the existing routes may stay and the possibility for a new sport climbing area might be realized.

GETTING THERE: From Idaho Falls, head north on I-15. Take exit 143 (Rexburg-Terreton), and drive west on State Highway 33. Pass through the towns of Terreton and Mud Lake and continue on until the T-intersection, turn left. Now head south for 4 miles then turn right. Drive west for 9 miles and turn right at the Simplot Farms sign. Head north on a gravel road for .5 mile, turn left onto 3600 N., head west for another .5 mile and turn right onto 1200 W. Continue north for 4 miles, the road turns into a good jeep track. After about 1 mile on the jeep track, signs about Box Canyon appear and there is a parking area to the right – low-clearance vehicles will want to park here. High-clearance vehicles can continue on – please make sure to stay on the road, there are small parking areas located by each crag – don't create new ones.

146

Dirt road entrance into Box Canyon.

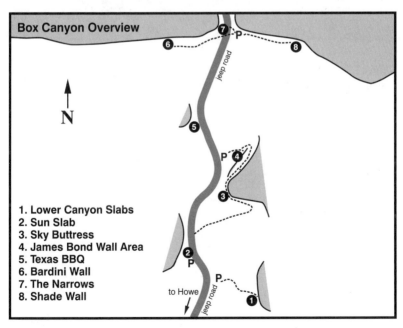

Box Canyon Overview

N

1. Lower Canyon Slabs
2. Sun Slab
3. Sky Buttress
4. James Bond Wall Area
5. Texas BBQ
6. Bardini Wall
7. The Narrows
8. Shade Wall

Lower Canyon slabs
(Morning shade, afternoon sun)

Routes are listed from left to right when facing wall.

1. Same As It Never Was (5.8)* – 4 bolts. Slab climb to steeper finish at chains. A little runout but easy. Can be set up as a toprope.

2. Wish List (5.7)** – 8 bolts. Fun slab climb to chains. Can be set up as a toprope.

3. It Ain't A Perfect World (5.8)* – 8 bolts. Start to the right of a big hole and cruise through fun moves to same anchors as Wish List.

148

A climber enjoys a stroll up Wish List, 5.7.

Sun Slab
(Morning sun, afternoon shade)

Routes are listed from left to right when facing wall.

1. Curious George (5.10c)** – 5 bolts. Steep climbing off the deck, route eases up after third bolt. Chain anchors.

2. The Grinch (5.9)* – 9 Bolts. Slab climb that eases up at midway anchors then steepens towards the end. Chains.

3. Ms. Rumphius (5.7)* – 5 bolts. Easy slab climb to chain anchors.

Sky Buttress

(Morning shade, afternoon sun)

Routes are listed from left to right when facing wall.

1. Hollowed Ground (5.11a)** – 8 bolts. Crux at start on rotten layer, merge with Corpolite at 6th bolt. Rappel anchors. 60m rope recommended.

2. While You're At It (5.10d) – Toprope.

3. Pocket Full of Corpolite (5.8)** – 8 bolts. Climb fun slabby face as it steepens at the top to end at rappel anchors. 60m rope recommended.

James Bond Wall Area

(Morning shade, afternoon shade)
Routes are listed from left to right when facing wall.

    1. McMeeken Route (5.12d)* – Bolts. Long, steep, thin climb up water streak.
    2. Oddjob (5.11c)*** – 3 bolts. Follow black bolts to cold shuts.
    3. Dr. No (5.12c/d)* – 3 bolts. Hard start, hard finish. Chain anchors.
    4. Thunderball (5.13a)** – 3 bolts. Steep and hard. Finishes on chains.
    5. Project (5.13+?) – 3 bolts. Good luck. Rap ring anchors.
    6. Barely Legal (5.11a)* – 5 bolts. Fun moves until crux by 5th bolt. Finish at
chain anchor.
    7. High Society (5.9) – Trad climb right leaning crack to the right of Barely
Legal. No anchors.

Texas BBQ Wall

Texas Barbeque
(Morning sun, afternoon shade)

Routes are listed from left to right when facing wall.

1. Texas Barbeque (5.12a)** – 5 bolts. Start up face to flake, then negotiate through the sharpest rock known to man. Chain anchors.

2. Weaner Dogs Ripped My Flesh (5.10c)** – 5 bolts. Fun route on sharp rock. Shares anchors with Texas.

3. Acupuncture Slab (5.9) – Toprope face just right of Weaner Dogs. Painfully sharp.

Bardini Wall

(Morning sun, afternoon sun)
Routes are listed from left to right when facing wall.

Matt Reymann finds Lemhi Winds (5.10a) a breeze.

1. Bardini Wall (5.10c/d)** – Pitch 1: (5.8) – Bolts. Starts to the left of big grassy ledge, below a bush. Go up past blocky shelf onto good face climbing and end on anchors at ledge. 90'. **Pitch 2: (5.10c/d)** – Bolts. Traverse leftward to balanced crux on pockets. Power up face while crimping to belay below horizontal white dike. 90'. **Pitch 3: (5.10a)** – Bolts. Continue up face on fun moves while taking advantage of good rest holds. Finish on anchors. 120'. Two ropes and about 16 quickdraws are required for this complete route.

2. The Coral Sea (5.10a)*** – 12 bolts. Start on grassy ledge, go up slab face, pass to the left of big hole. Cruise through roof section on positive holds and finish on diagonal pockets at chain anchors. An awesome route at 150'; two ropes are needed for rappel.

The Narrows, left side
(Morning sun, afternoon shade)
Routes are listed from left to right when facing wall.

1. Lemhi Winds (5.10a)* – 7 bolts. Start just left of big flake, breeze through face on fun moves to undercling and finish on positive holds at chains.

2. The Thread (5.12c)* – 10 bolts. Start just to the right of flake, up to ledge and first crux. Crimp to good holds, clip the threaded sling, then fire second, thin crux to chain anchors. 60m rope is needed.

Shade Wall

(Morning shade, afternoon shade)
Routes are listed from left to right when facing wall.

1. Unnamed (5.10b)** – Pitch 1: (5.7) – Bolts. Fun pitch that angles slightly right to chain anchors. 80'. **Pitch 2 : (5.9)** – Bolts. From chains veer right then up past horizontal seams to chain anchors below big ledge. 60'. **Pitch 3: (5.10b)** – Bolts. Traverse left then up face to chain anchors. 75'. 16 quickdraws and two ropes are required.

2. Unnamed (5.11a)*** – Pitch 1: (5.9) – Bolts. Climb orange water streak to chain anchors. 195'. **Pitch 2: (5.11a)** – Bolts. Start off veering slightly left, through thin section, then diagonally right through second crux and finish on chain anchors. 160'. 16 quickdraws and two ropes are necessary.

Jerry Painter climbs route 18 on a fine March day at Darby Wall.

DARBY CANYON

Located on the west side of the Teton range just outside of Driggs, Darby Canyon offers climbers a little taste of some great limestone sport climbing. A fine alternative to the smooth, slopey climbs just to the north in Teton Canyon, Darby Wall is similar to the limestone in Box Canyon. Darby Wall hosts climbs that range from 5.7 – 5.11+. Slabby, textured limestone comprise the current routes, but there are room and plans for harder, steeper lines. Development began in 2002 by the Olsen brothers of the Teton Valley area. The routes did not have any names at press time.

GETTING THERE: From Idaho Falls, head north on Highway 20 to Rexburg. Just north of Rexburg, take the exit for Highway 33 and travel east to the town of Driggs. Continue past Driggs for about 2 miles and turn left onto Darby Road, (there is a sign reading "Darby Canyon"). Follow the pavement as it gives way to a gravel road, take the right fork in the road. At about 1.3 miles up the gravel road, park at the trailhead for the Aspen trail, (signed 034), on the left. Follow the trail for about 40 yards, then take the narrow right fork up the hill and continue on for about 200 yards. Darby Wall is on the left.

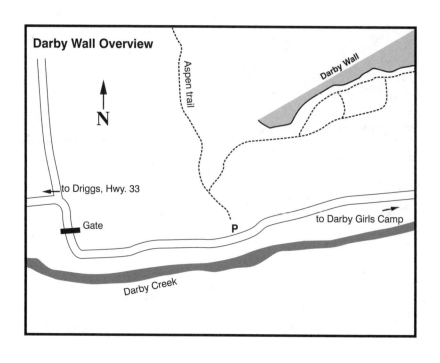

Darby Wall Overview

N

to Driggs, Hwy. 33

Gate

Aspen trail

Darby Wall

P

to Darby Girls Camp

Darby Creek

To Routes 2-19 ▷

xx

1

Darby Wall
(Morning sun, late afternoon shade)

Developed by Troy Olsen and friends in the Teton Valley. Routes are listed from left to right when facing wall.

1. 5.10a* – 7 bolts. Angle right and up to big flake by 4th bolt, then finish on left side of bolt line. A big hold broke at the 2nd bolt, bumping the grade up a notch to .10a. Chain anchors.

The following routes are located about 80 yards to the right of route 1.

2. 5.9* – 4 bolts. Up slabby face to crux at mid-route, then finish on crimps and good holds. Chain anchors.

3. 5.10a* – 5 bolts. Start on easy slab, first bolt is way up there. Crimp to small underclings, then finish on good holds. Chain anchors.

4. 5.9** – 5 bolts. Start directly below the first bolt, crimp, side pull and pinch your way to chain anchors.

Mike Benson cruises up route 5 at Darby Wall.

5. 5.7* – 5 bolts. Climb easy, slabby face. Good beginner route. Chain anchors.

6. 5.10c* – 6 bolts. Spicy start to vertical seam, finish on good holds. Chain anchors.

7. 5.10b*** – 6 bolts. Crux low on route, eases up after 3rd bolt. Chain anchors.

8. 5.11c** – 7 bolts. Start directly below first bolt, move up and over roof to big rest ledge, then up smooth, vertical face, finish on good pockets. Chain anchors.

9. 5.11d*** – 6 bolts. Powerful, bouldery start to big holds then finish at roof. A quality route! Rap ring anchors.

Matt TeNgaio reaches for a clip on route 8 at Darby Wall.

161

10. 5.11b/c* – 6 bolts. Located near small staircase. Sustained route. Chain anchors.

11. 5.7* – 3 bolts. Short, easy route. Chain anchors.

12. 5.11a** – 6 bolts. Fun route with crux up high. Chain anchors.

13. 5.10c/d* – 4 bolts. Chain anchors.

14. 5.10a** – 5 bolts. More crimpy, slabby fun. Chain anchors.

15. 5.10b/c* – 4 bolts. Chain anchors.

16. 5.10c/d* – 4 bolts. Chain anchors.

17. 5.11a/b* – 6 bolts. Chain anchors.

18. 5.10c/d** – 5 bolts. Couple of ways to start this one. Main crux higher up. Moving out right at 4th bolt helps. Chain anchors.

19. 5.11d/.12a* – 8 bolts. Start below small roof, then angle slightly left over roof. Chain anchors.

Located in one of the most beautiful settings in the region, Teton Canyon has plenty to offer in the way of rock climbing. Originally climbed traditionally for years, the Grand Wall became the Teton Valley hotspot for hard sport climbing in the late '80s to early '90s.

While the Grand Wall has recently seen additional development, walls like the Slim Shady Wall are also being discovered and developed – proof that this canyon is hardly close to being tapped out.

GETTING THERE: From Driggs, turn east on Little Avenue/Ski Hill Road and go about 6 miles and turn right onto Teton Canyon Road, which quickly turns to dirt. Drive about 3.5 miles to the end of the road. Take the south fork trail, which starts just right of the bathrooms, and immediately look for a smaller trail leading left to the big granite formation. Arms Deal Wall is to the left and up.

For access to the Slim Shady Wall walk to the campground and walk south past campsite No. 7 toward the cliffs and cross the creek.

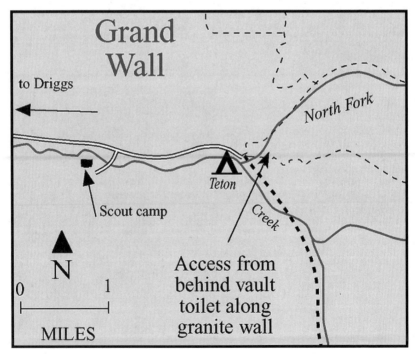

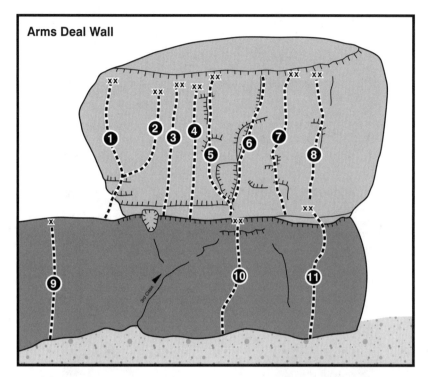

Arms Deal Wall
(Morning shade, afternoon sun)

Overhung wall located left and up of the Grand Wall. Routes are listed from left to right when facing wall.

1. **G1 (5.12b)*** – Bolts. Anchors.
2. **G2 (5.12c)** – Bolts. Anchors.
3. **G3 (5.14) project**
4. **G4 (5.14) project**
5. **Arms Deal (5.13 b)*** – Bolts. Anchors.
6. **Munger Crack (5.11c)*** – Gear. No anchors.
7. **Jaimé Hole (5.12a)*** – Bolts. Anchors.
8. **Holey Moley (5.11b/c)*** – Bolts. Anchors.
9. **Toprope (5.7)** – Anchors.
10. **Rat Hole (5.12a/b)** – Bolts. Anchors.
11. **Dr. Hole (5.12a)*** – Bolts. Anchors.

Sam Painter on Thumper, Grand Wall.

A climber starting up Z-Crack, 5.9.

Z-Crack Area
(Morning shade, afternoon sun)

Located between Arms Deal Wall and Grand Wall. Indentified by prominent "Z" crack feature. No topo.

1. Lady Killer (5.11b)* – Bolts/Gear. 2 rope rappel. Climbs the first half of Z-Crack then heads left and finshes on bolts. Anchors.

4. Z Crack (5.9)** – Gear. Starts in dihedral to grassy ledge, then follows obvious "Z-Crack" feature. 2 rope rappel. Anchors.

A climber enjoys a run up the 5.9 Crack, Grand Wall.

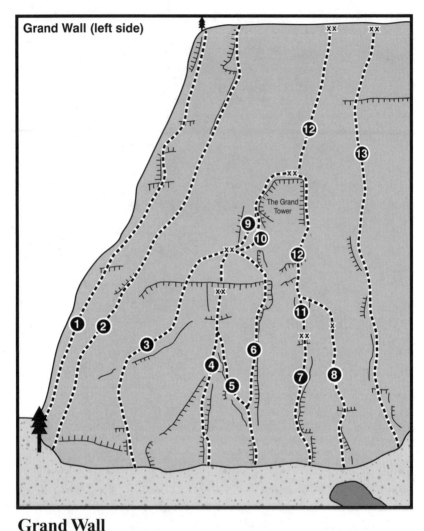

Grand Wall (left side)

The Grand Tower

Grand Wall
(Morning shade, afternoon sun)

Big obvious wall just to the left at the start of the Teton Canyon south fork trail. Routes are listed from left to right when facing wall.

1. Thimbleberry (5.5R)* – Gear. Route starts about 10' left of Double Cracks. Climb straight up. No Anchors.
2. Double Cracks (5.7)* – Gear. Starts near a tree at the base of the wall. Climb up and slightly right. No Anchors.
3. Slope on a Rope: (5.11c) *** – Bolts. Route angles right and ends on ledge with anchors directly above Bambi and Thumper.
4. Bambi (5.11b)** – Bolts. Anchors.

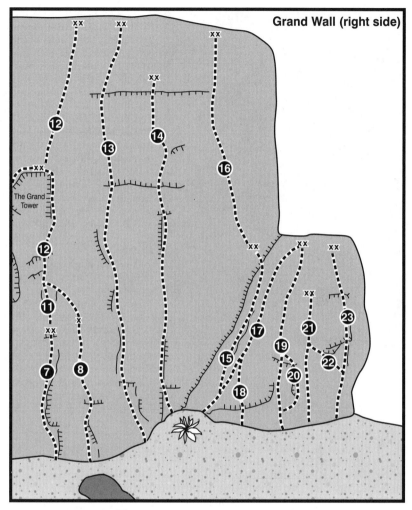

5. Thumper (5.11c) – Bolts. Merges with Bambi partway up.

6. Moonlight (5.12c/d) – Bolts/Fixed pins. Direct finish to Thumper.

7. S.O.S. (5.10c) – Bolts.

8. Super Slab (5.12b) – Bolts. Single biner marks the anchors. 5.13 project above that meges with Guides Wail.

9. I.Q. Test (5.10a)* – Bolts/Gear. Starts on anchors above Bambi and Thumper. Starts on bolts then requires gear as it ascends the left side of the Grand Tower.

10. Original Route (5.9)* – Gear. Walk to the right side of ledge and climb to merge with I.Q. Test.

11. Guides Wail (5.13c)* – Bolts. Continuation pitch after S.O.S. Technically no anchors but can combine 1st pitch of The Proud to reach anchors on top of the Grand Tower.

169

Scott Babbit nears the anchors on Z-Crack.
Photo by Jim Olson.

12. The Prowd (5.11b)* – **Pitch 1: (5.11a)** – Bolts/Gear. To access this route climb S.O.S., then if you're feeling spunky climb Guide's Wail OR just aid through the 5.13 section to the 5.8 section which signifies the start of The Prowd. Climb the right side of the Grand Tower. May want a #2 Camelot for the top of the pitch. **Pitch 2: (5.11b)** – Bolts. Starts at the top of the Grand Tower. Two single rope raps to get down of walk off to the left. Anchors.

13. Mayday (5.12a)*** – Bolts. Two rope rappel. Anchors.

14. High Noon (5.11d)*** – Bolts. Two rope rappel. Anchors.

15. 5.9 Crack (5.9)** – Gear. Original start is in the same corner where High Noon starts, although, more commonly started on Slabadellic, then veer slightly left to crack after first bolt on Slabadellic. Anchors

16. Afternoon Delight (5.12b)* – Bolts. Continuation pitch after 5.9 Crack. Two rope rappel. Anchors.

17. Slabadellic: (5.9)*** – Bolts. Shares anchors with Uzi-Waza.

18. Full Sail (5.12d/.13a)** – Bolts. Shares anchors with Uzi-Waza.

19. Uzi-Waza (5.12a)* – Bolts. Anchors.

20. Uzi-Waza Variation (5.10c)** – Bolts. Same start but head right about 8' up over to lone bolt, then up to bypass .12a crux, then merge left again.

21. Kinjite (5.11c)* – Bolts. Anchors.

22. Ninjitsu (5.11b)* – Bolts. Starts on Sepekku then heads left to merge with Kinjite.

23. Sepekku (5.11d/.12a)** – Bolts. Right-most route on the wall. Anchors.

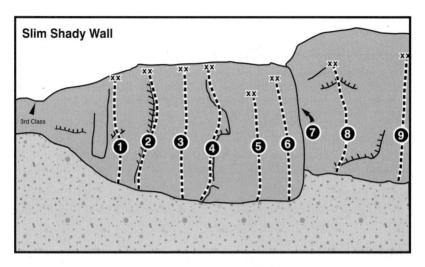

Slim Shady Wall
(All day shade)

Located about 300 feet south of campsite No. 7 across the creek. Wall is accessed by crossing the creek via logs and game trail. Some are bolted, some are not and some are mixed – use your better judgement before leaving the ground. Routes are listed from left to right when facing wall.

1. **Warm up (5.10c)****
2. **Brady's Crack (5.12b)*****
3. **Project (5.13)**
4. **Classic Corner (5.11b/c)*****
5. **Flowstone 1 (5.10d)***.
6. **Flowstone 2 (5.10d/11a)**
7. **Project**
8. **Slim Shady (5.12c)***** Moves through 2 roofs.
9. **Project**

BOULDERING AREAS

The problems at the areas listed here are mainly elimination problems, to list them all requires an independent guide book of its own. For the diehard boulderer, make the 2^1/$_2$-hour drive from Idaho Falls to Dierkes Lake in Twin Falls for endless, stellar problems (not to mention the killer sport routes there!).

Wave Wall

Located on the southeast end of Pocatello south of Century High School off the north side of Interstate 15, this overhung wall offers a handful of fun problems.

Ross Park

The same cliffs that sport climbers use also make for a smorgasbord of fun problems. The majority of problems lie on the Shady Side.

Badger Creek

Located north of Tetonia, on the north end of the Teton Valley. About .5 mile up Badger Creek Road, numerous boulders can be found with established problems. A crash pad is helpful out here.

The Dam Boulders

In the Teton River Canyon about a mile downstream from the old dam site northeast of Newdale, Idaho is a cluster of boulders. There are several problems that feature good movement and nice landings.

OTHER CLIMBING AREAS OF INTEREST

In order to keep this guide book as local to the eastern Snake River Valley as possible, we've decided to omit areas in Jackson and the massive sport climbing area of Massacre Rocks – guide books are available for these and adjoining areas. Here is a list of other crags in the region.

• **Massacre Rocks** – Located west of American Falls with more than 300 bolted routes on great basalt.

• **Rodeo Wall** – Follow Highway 89 past Palisades Reservoir heading east – turn left at Alpine Junction and continue up the scenic Snake River Canyon. Limestone crag to the left at mile marker 139.

• **Hoback Shield** – About 11 miles east past the Hoback Junction near Jackson, Wyo., this limestone crag sits left above Highway 189. Hosting mainly .9s and .10s, a good place for the intermediate lead climber.

• **Blacktail Butte** – Just 12 miles north of Jackson, Wyo., this dead vertical limestone wall offers thin test pieces for the aspiring 5.12 leader. It's suggested the ratings here are a bit sandbagged.

• **Corbet's & S&S Couloirs** – Take the tram at Teton Village Ski Resort to the top. The couloirs are located downhill from the big bulletin board and just below the out-of-bounds signs posted atop the couloirs. Rappel to get to the base of the cliffs. Development continues in this area. Routes mainly in the 5.11 to 5.13 range.

172

Useful Addresses and Phone numbers

Caribou-Targhee National Forest
■ Ashton Ranger District, Box 228, 30 South Yellowstone Highway, Ashton, ID 83420, (208) 652-7442
■ Dubois Ranger District, P.O. Box 46, Dubois, ID 83423 (208) 374-5422
■ Island Park Ranger District, P.O. Box 220, Island Park, ID 83429, (208) 558-7301
■ Palisades Ranger District, 3659 East Ririe Highway, Idaho Falls, ID 83401 (208) 523-1412
■ Teton Basin Ranger District, P.O. Box 777, Driggs, ID 83422, (208) 354-2312
■ Malad Ranger District, 75 South 140 East, P.O. Box 142, Malad, ID 83262 (208) 766-4743
■ Montpelier Ranger District, 431 Clay, Montpelier, ID 83254, (208) 847-0375.
■ Pocatello Ranger District, Federal Building, Suite 187, 250 South 4th Avenue, Pocatello, ID 83201, (208) 236-7500
■ Soda Springs Ranger District, 421 West 2nd South, Soda Springs, ID 83276, (208) 547-4356

State Parks
■ Harriman State Park, HC-66 Box 500, Island Park, ID 83429, (208) 558-7368
■ Massacre Rocks State Park, 3592 N. Park Lane, American Falls, ID 83211, (208) 548-2672

Bureau of Land Management
■ Idaho Falls office,1405 Hollipark Drive, Idaho Falls, ID 83401, (208) 524-7500

Other agencies
■ Department of Recreation, City of Pocatello, P.O. Box 4169, Pocatello, ID 83205-4169, (208) 234-6232

Idaho Falls Ski Club
■ Web site: www.ifskiclub.com/

Idaho Alpine Club
■ Web site: www.idahoalpineclub.org

Idaho State University Outdoor Program
■ Web site: www.isu.edu/outdoor

Southeast Idaho climbing Web site
■ Web site: www.seiclimbing.com

Matt TeNgaio, left, and Jerry Painter on the summit of the South Teton in May 2004.

ABOUT THE AUTHORS

Matt TeNgaio works as a graphic artist at the Post Register newspaper. When he isn't sitting on his duff pretending to work, he can be found scouting for future crags in the summer or in the backcountry skiing/snowboarding during the winter months and has a weakness for Nutter Butters. He lives in Idaho Falls with his wife and two kids. He can be contacted at mtengaio@postregister.com.

Jerry Painter has lived in Idaho Falls since 1988 with his wife and family. He is an outdoor columnist for the Post Register newspaper. He enjoys being scared to death on top of the region's highest peaks and keeping up with his children on their latest 5.11 projects. His other books include "Great Trails for Family Hiking: The Tetons" (out of print), "10 Peaks in 10 Weeks" and "Trails of Eastern Idaho" with Margaret Fuller. He can be contacted at jpainter@postregister.com.